EDITORIAL STAFF

Vice President and Editor-in-Chief: Anne Van Wagner Childs
Executive Director: Sandra Graham Case
Editorial Director: Susan Frantz Wiles
Publications Director: Carla Bentley
Creative Art Director: Gloria Bearden
Senior Graphics Art Director: Melinda Stout

DESIGN
Design Director: Patricia Wallenfang Sowers
Designers: Katherine Prince Horton, Sandra Spotts Ritchie,
    Linda Diehl Tiano, and Rebecca Sunwall Werle
Executive Assistant: Billie Steward
Design Assistants: Sharon Heckel Gillam and
    Barbara Bryant Scott

TECHNICAL
Managing Editor: Kathy Rose Bradley
Technical Editor: Leslie Schick Gorrell
Senior Technical Writer: Kimberly J. Smith
Technical Writers: Margaret F. Cox, Briget Julia
    Laskowski, and Kristine Anderson Mertes
Technical Associate: Carol A. Reed

EDITORIAL
Managing Editor: Linda L. Trimble
Associate Editor: Robyn Sheffield-Edwards
Assistant Editors: Tammi Williamson Bradley,
    Terri Leming Davidson, and Darla Burdette Kelsay
Copy Editor: Laura Lee Weland

ART
Book/Magazine Graphics Art Director: Diane M. Hugo
Senior Graphics Illustrator: Michael A. Spigner
Photography Stylists: Sondra Daniel, Karen Smart Hall,
    Aurora Huston, Christina Tiano Myers, Zaneta Senger,
    and Alaina Sokora

PROMOTIONS
Managing Editors: Tena Kelley Vaughn and
    Marjorie Ann Lacy
Associate Editors: Steven M. Cooper, Marla Shivers,
    Dixie L. Morris, and Jennifer Leigh Ertl
Designer: Rhonda H. Hestir
Art Director: Linda Lovette Smart
Production Artist: Leslie Loring Krebs
Publishing Systems Administrator: Cindy Lumpkin
Publishing Systems Assistant: Susan Mary Gray

BUSINESS STAFF

Publisher: Bruce Akin
Vice President, Finance: Tom Siebenmorgen
Vice President, Retail Sales: Thomas L. Carlisle
Retail Sales Director: Richard Tignor
Vice President, Retail Marketing: Pam Stebbins
Retail Marketing Director: Margaret Sweetin
Retail Customer Services Manager: Carolyn Pruss

General Merchandise Manager: Russ Barnett
Distribution Director: Ed M. Strackbein
Vice President, Marketing: Guy A. Crossley
Marketing Manager: Byron L. Taylor
Print Production Manager: Laura Lockhart
Print Production Coordinator: Nancy Reddick Baker

Library of Congress Catalog Number 96-77625
International Standard Book Number 1-57486-048-8

Trash TO TREASURE

*W*ant to discover hidden treasures beyond imagination?
Then use Trash to Treasure *as your secret map to crafty "recycled"
riches! Buried beneath your empty detergent boxes, wallpaper scraps,
fabric remnants, egg cartons, and chipped cups and saucers lies a
fortune in unique handmade gifts, home accessories, holiday
decorations, and much more. You'll find over 140 delightful ways to
transform everyday discards into dazzling dandies that are as good
as gold! Divided into four exciting collections, this invaluable guide
includes Holiday Magic for all through the year, Great Gifts for
everyone you hold dear, Home Sweet Spruce-Ups for dressing up your
decor, and Fun Fix-Ups that even youngsters can help make. Lots
of "before" photographs show some of the items you'll need to craft
these clever creations. You'll achieve perfect results every time with
our easy-to-follow directions and full-color photographs. Made from
items that you would ordinarily throw away, these one-of-a-kind
projects will not only save you money, but will also help save our
environment. So set sail on a crafting adventure to a wonderful
new world of creative recycling with* Trash to Treasure!

Anne Childs

LEISURE ARTS, INC.
Little Rock, Arkansas

TABLE OF CONTENTS

Holiday MAGIC 6

Great GIFTS 34

TABLE OF CONTENTS

Home Sweet SPRUCE-UPS 60

TABLE OF CONTENTS

Fun FIX-UPS 90

Holiday
MAGIC

Show off your holiday spirit at Christmas and throughout the year with unique home decorations and clever gift containers made from items you would ordinarily throw away! It's fun, it's easy, and it's inexpensive. You'll discover fanciful projects, from nostalgic handmade valentines to candle holders for Christmas — not to mention novel whatnots such as patriotic luminarias made from metal cans, spooky bottled Halloween favors, an Easter wreath featuring crushed can bunnies, and a Thanksgiving table runner stamped with natural motifs.

*B*eautiful tokens of your affection, these fanciful valentines are crafted from old calendars. To coordinate, purchased envelopes are decorated inside and out with nostalgic snippets. The large envelope is simply a whole calendar page that's folded, glued together at the sides, and lined with a lacy paper doily. Sentimental souls will adore these vintage greetings!

VICTORIAN VALENTINES

Recycled item: either a wall calendar or wrapping paper with Victorian motifs.
You will also need: a craft glue stick.
For raised-motif card with envelope, you will also need: a 6¼" x 9" piece of stationery paper, a 6"w heart-shaped paper doily, an 8" round paper doily, and double-sided foam tape.
For each note card and envelope, you will also need: a plain card with envelope to match, paper lace, and a gold paint pen with extra-fine point.
For heart-shaped valentine, you will also need: a 6¼" x 9" piece of stationery paper, a 6"w heart-shaped paper doily, and 20" of ⅝"w wired ribbon.
For gift card and envelope, you will also need: desired color paper for card and a small envelope to match.

RAISED-MOTIF CARD WITH ENVELOPE

1. For card, match short edges and fold stationery paper piece in half (outside of folded paper is outside of card); unfold paper piece and place on work surface with outside up and short edges at top and bottom. Center heart-shaped doily upside down on paper piece so bottom of heart extends 1½" above fold line (Fig. 1); glue in place. Refold paper piece.

Fig. 1

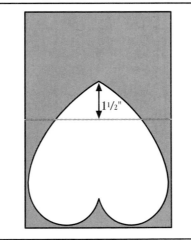

2. Cutting through both layers, trim paper close to edges of doily on front of card.
3. For background motifs, cut desired motifs from calendar. Glue motifs to card.
4. For raised motifs, cut desired motifs from calendar. Apply small pieces of foam tape to backs of motifs. Remove paper backing from tape and apply motifs to front of card. (*Note:* To raise motifs higher, use more than 1 layer of tape.)
5. For envelope, cut an 8½" x 11¼" paper piece from calendar. Position and glue round doily on back of paper piece (inside of envelope) to cover any writing.
6. Fold bottom edge of paper piece 4¾" to back to form envelope. Glue side edges together. For flap, fold top edge of paper piece down 1¼".

NOTE CARDS AND ENVELOPES

1. (*Note:* Follow all steps for each note card and envelope.) For note card, trim ¼" from edges of card.
2. Cut pieces from paper lace to fit along edges of front of card. With edges of lace pieces extending about ¼" beyond edges of card, glue lace pieces along edges on inside front of card.
3. Cut desired motifs from calendar for front of card. Glue motifs to card.
4. Either use paint pen and a ruler to draw a border about ¼" inside edges on front of card or use paint pen to draw around motifs on card.
5. For envelope liner, place envelope with flap open over desired motif on calendar page; draw around envelope. Cut shape from paper about ⅛" inside drawn lines. Place paper piece in envelope. Trim paper piece to expose gummed edge of envelope flap. Glue paper piece in envelope.

HEART-SHAPED VALENTINE

1. Glue center of doily to stationery paper. Cutting about ⅛" from doily, cut doily from paper.
2. Cut motifs from calendar and glue to doily. Glue 1 or more motifs to paper heart under edge of doily with motifs extending beyond edges of heart.
3. Tie ribbon into a bow; trim ends. Glue bow and streamers to heart as desired. Cut a motif from calendar and glue to bow.

GIFT CARD AND ENVELOPE

1. For card, measure height of closed envelope; subtract ¼" and multiply by 2. Measure width of envelope; subtract ¼". Cut a piece of paper the determined measurements. Matching short edges, fold paper piece in half.
2. Cut desired motifs from calendar. Glue motifs to card and envelope, overlapping motifs as desired and trimming motifs even with edges of card as necessary.

SWEETHEART BOXES

A sweet surprise awaits your beloved when valentine treasures are tucked inside these pretty gift containers! Wrapped in romance, small painted boxes in various shapes are embellished with newspaper roses and elegant bows.

Recycled items: newspaper and small boxes (we used a fast-food sandwich box, a check box, and a heart-shaped candy box).

You will also need: white, light pink, dark pink, and burgundy acrylic paint; small sponge pieces; paper towels; silk leaves; floral wire; wire cutters; desired ribbon(s); 1/8" dia. gold twisted cord (optional); a low-temperature hot glue gun and glue sticks; and desired gift to place in box.

For gold box, you will also need: gold acrylic spray paint.

For sponge-painted box, you will also need: white acrylic spray paint and metallic gold acrylic paint.

1. (*Note:* Either spray paint box gold or follow Step 1 to sponge paint box.) Spray paint box white. Dip a dampened sponge piece into light pink paint; remove excess on a paper towel. Using a light stamping motion, use sponge piece to paint box; allow to dry. Repeat, using clean sponge pieces and dark pink, then gold paint.

2. For roses, unfold 1 newspaper page and lay flat. Dip a clean dampened sponge piece into white paint; remove excess on a paper towel. Using a light stamping motion so newsprint shows through, use sponge piece to paint newspaper; allow to dry. Repeat with light pink, dark pink, and burgundy paint as desired, using more of light paint colors for lighter roses and more of dark paint colors for darker roses.

3. (*Note:* Follow Steps 3 - 5 for each rose.) Cut either a 4" x 14" strip for large rose or a 4" x 7" strip for small rose from sponge-painted paper.

4. Fold 1 end of strip 1/4" to wrong side. Matching wrong sides, fold paper strip in half lengthwise (long folded edge is top of strip).

5. Beginning with unfolded end, roll about one-quarter of strip tightly to form rose center; glue to secure. To form petals, wrap bottom edge of strip around rose center, folding small uneven pleats in bottom edge, bending top edge outward slightly, and spot gluing bottom edge in place as necessary. At end of strip, fold strip diagonally toward rose center; glue to secure. Wire stems of leaves to bottoms of roses.

6. Place gift in box.

7. Either tie ribbon(s) into a bow around box or glue a length of ribbon around box and then glue on a separate bow; trim ends. If desired, tie a length of cord into a bow, knot and fray each end, and glue cord bow to center of ribbon bow on box.

8. Arrange roses on box as desired; glue in place.

CUTE EASTER CANS

A fun change from the traditional Easter basket, our cute treat canisters are ideal for holding colorful eggs, wrapped candies, and lots more. "Recycled" from empty food cans, these happy keepers are Earth-friendly, too!

HAPPY EASTER TREAT CANS

Recycled items: 1/2- and 1-pound coffee cans, a wire coat hanger, and four large buttons.

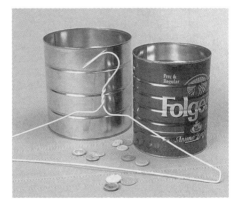

You will also need: masking tape (if needed), either tissue paper or fabric to line can, and a hot glue gun and glue sticks.

For Easter egg can, you will also need: white spray paint, assorted colors of craft foam for eggs, assorted colors of acrylic paint for dots, pencils with unused erasers, 2 colors of jumbo rickrack, 2/3 yd of 7/8"w ribbon, pliers, wire cutters, hammer, large nail or nail punch, and tracing paper.

For bunny can, you will also need: light blue spray paint, white and pink craft foam, assorted colors of acrylic paint for dots, pencils with unused erasers, 16 1/2" of 7/8"w ribbon, black permanent felt-tip pen with fine point, tracing paper, and graphite transfer paper.

For "Happy Easter!" can, you will also need: pink spray paint, white and pink craft foam, baby rickrack, and a black permanent felt-tip pen with fine point.

EASTER EGG CAN

1. For handle, use pliers to untwist coat hanger and straighten wire; cut an 18" length from wire. Use hammer and nail to make a hole near rim on each side of can. Insert 1 end of wire into each hole and bend ends up to secure.
2. If necessary, use masking tape to cover sharp edge inside top of can.
3. Spray paint can and handle white.
4. Glue rickrack around top and bottom of can.
5. Trace egg pattern, shown in blue on page 120, onto tracing paper; cut out. Use pattern to cut desired number of eggs from craft foam.
6. Glue eggs to can.
7. For dots, use pencil erasers dipped in paint to paint dots on eggs and can.
8. Tie ribbon into a bow around handle; trim ends.
9. Line can with tissue paper.

BUNNY CAN

1. If necessary, use masking tape to cover sharp edge inside top of can.
2. Spray paint can light blue.
3. For dots, use pencil erasers dipped in paint to paint dots on can.
4. Trace head outline, inner ears, and nose of bunny pattern, shown in blue on page 120, separately onto tracing paper; cut out. Use patterns to cut head from white craft foam and inner ears and nose from pink craft foam.
5. Trace remaining features of bunny pattern, shown in grey on page 120, onto tracing paper. Use transfer paper to transfer features to head. Use black pen to draw over transferred features.
6. Glue inner ears and nose to head.
7. For bow tie, cut one 7", one 6", and one 2 1/2" length from ribbon. Overlap ends of 7" length 1" to form a loop; glue to secure. Repeat with 6" length. With overlaps at center back, stack small loop on large loop. Wrap 2 1/2" ribbon length around centers of loops; glue ends at back to secure.
8. Glue bunny and bow tie to can.
9. Line can with tissue paper.

"HAPPY EASTER!" CAN

1. If necessary, use masking tape to cover sharp edge inside top of can.
2. Spray paint can pink.
3. Cut a 2" x 1" piece of pink craft foam and a 3 1/2" x 2 1/4" piece of white craft foam.
4. Use black pen to write "Happy Easter!" on pink foam piece. Glue pink foam piece to center of white foam piece.
5. Glue lengths of rickrack along center of white foam piece border. Thread a length of rickrack through holes in each button and glue ends to back of button.
6. Glue buttons to corners of white foam piece. Glue foam piece to can.
7. Line can with tissue paper.

BUNNY TRAIL WREATH

Celebrate Easter with our whimsical accent — it's hopping with personality! To make it, a grapevine wreath is embellished with painted plastic foam eggs, carefree crushed can bunnies, and a wired-ribbon bow. Tiny silk flowers and asparagus fern give the wreath springtime charm.

EASTER WREATH

Recycled items: 12-ounce aluminum beverage cans and foam food trays.

You will also need: a 20" dia. grapevine wreath, dried asparagus fern, assorted small silk flowers, white spray paint, small paintbrushes, 2 yds of 2¹/₂"w wired ribbon, 6" of floral wire, tracing paper, and a hot glue gun and glue sticks.

For each bunny, you will also need: white spray primer; white, pink, red, and light blue acrylic paint; white craft foam; a ¹/₂" dia. pink pom-pom for nose; a 1" dia. white pom-pom for tail; 12" of 1"w satin ribbon; black permanent felt-tip pen with fine point; and graphite transfer paper.

For each Easter egg, you will also need: white gesso; assorted colors of acrylic paint; foam brushes; cotton swabs, toothpicks, and rickrack (optional); and a craft knife and cutting mat or folded newspaper.

1. Spray paint wreath white.
2. (*Note:* Follow Steps 2 - 8 for each bunny. Refer to Fig. 1 for Step 2.) Remove pop-top from can. To bend can, use both hands to hold can with thumbs below top rim and opening to 1 side (Fig. 1 shows a crushed can for a left-facing bunny). Using thumbs to press on can, bend top rim down. Turn can upside down and repeat for bottom rim, pressing on opposite side of can. Use foot to further flatten can.

Fig. 1

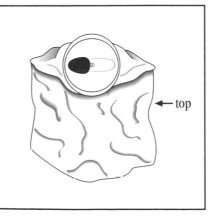

← top

3. Spray can with primer, then white spray paint.
4. For mouth, paint inside of can behind opening red. Dilute pink paint with water. Use fingertip to paint cheeks on can.
5. Trace eyes pattern, page 120, onto tracing paper. Use transfer paper to transfer eyes to can (for eyes looking right, turn traced pattern over before transferring eyes). Paint irises light blue. Paint white highlights in eyes. Use black pen to draw over transferred lines and draw whiskers on can.
6. For ears and teeth, trace patterns, page 120, onto tracing paper. Use patterns to cut teeth and 2 ears from craft foam. Use pink paint to paint each inner ear. Use black pen to draw a line at center of teeth. Glue ears to top of head; glue tab at top of teeth inside mouth.
7. Glue pink and white pom-poms to bunny for nose and tail.
8. Tie satin ribbon length into a bow; trim ends. Glue bow to bunny.
9. Trace egg patterns, shown in black on page 120, onto tracing paper; cut out. Use patterns and craft knife to cut desired number of eggs from foam trays.
10. Use a foam brush to apply gesso to eggs.
11. Use a clean foam brush and acrylic paint to paint desired basecoat color on each egg.
12. Paint designs on eggs as desired. (We painted stripes and dots on our eggs. For wavy stripes, we used a pencil to draw around lengths of rickrack on eggs, then filled in stripes with paint. We used cotton swabs and toothpicks to paint large and small dots.)
13. Follow *Making a Multi-Loop Bow*, page 127, to make a double-loop bow with center loop from wired ribbon.
14. Arrange fern, flowers, eggs, bunnies, and bow on wreath; glue to secure.

EASTER SURPRISE BOX

*O*ur unique Easter gift box is super easy to make! A clear plastic food container is simply painted pink and topped with colorful funny-paper posies and a polka-dot bow.

EASTER GIFT BOX

Recycled items: small plastic food container and color comics from newspaper.

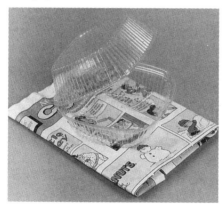

You will also need: ⁷⁄₈ yd of ⁷⁄₈"w ribbon, desired color floral spray paint, floral wire, wire cutters, green floral tape, tracing paper, and a low-temperature hot glue gun and glue sticks.

1. Spray paint container.
2. (*Note:* Follow Steps 2 - 4 to make 2 roses.) Trace petal pattern, page 120, onto tracing paper; cut out. Use pattern to cut 6 petals from comics. Wrap top edges of each petal around a pencil to curl (Fig. 1).

Fig. 1

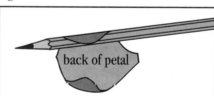
back of petal

3. For rose center, cut a 3" x 13" strip from comics. Fold 1 end of strip ¹⁄₄" to 1 side (wrong side). Matching wrong sides, fold strip in half lengthwise (long folded edge is top of strip). Beginning with unfolded end, roll about one quarter of strip tightly; glue to secure. Roll remainder of strip loosely, folding small uneven pleats in bottom edge and spot gluing bottom edge to secure.

4. With top edges curling outward, wrap bottom of 1 petal around bottom of rose center; glue to secure. Wrap a second petal around rose center opposite first petal; glue to secure. Overlapping petals, repeat to glue remaining petals around rose center.
5. For stem on each rose, glue 1 end of a 2" length of floral wire into bottom of rose. Wrap bottom of rose and wire with floral tape, covering wire completely.
6. Follow *Making a Multi-Loop Bow*, page 127, to make a double-loop bow from ribbon.
7. Arrange roses and bow on box as desired; glue in place.

PATRIOTIC PLACE MAT

*A*dd all-American flair to your Fourth of July picnic with novel place mats made from paper grocery bags. Decorated with fused-on fabric appliqués, the place mats can be covered with clear self-adhesive plastic for easy cleanups and years of use. Friends and family will salute your thrifty ingenuity!

PATRIOTIC PLACE MAT

Recycled item: paper grocery bag.
You will also need: fabrics for background and star appliqués, paper-backed fusible web, and clear self-adhesive plastic (Con-tact® paper; optional).

1. Cut a 16½" x 11½" piece from bag; use a dry iron to press paper piece flat.
2. For background appliqué, follow manufacturer's instructions to fuse web to wrong side of fabric for background. Cut a 14" x 9" piece from fabric.

3. For star appliqués, trace star pattern, page 122, 4 times onto paper side of web. Follow manufacturer's instructions to fuse web to wrong side of fabric for stars; cut out appliqués along drawn lines.
4. Remove paper backing from background and stars. Center background on paper piece and arrange stars over corners; fuse in place.

5. For a more durable place mat, cut a piece of self-adhesive plastic slightly larger than place mat; remove paper backing. Place place mat right side down on adhesive plastic and press in place. Trim plastic even with edges of place mat. If desired, repeat to cover back of place mat.

AMERICAN STAR LIGHTS

Whether used poolside or on the patio table, these patriotic luminarias and candle holders are a fitting tribute for a star-spangled holiday. Crafted from empty cans, they're an inexpensive way to light up your Independence Day celebration.

SPIRITED CANDLE HOLDERS

Recycled items: assorted large cans with lids for punched candle holders (we used 1- to 3-pound coffee cans); assorted small cans for appliquéd candle holders; a single serving-size plastic beverage bottle with lid; and red, white, and blue buttons (optional).

You will also need: tracing paper.
For fireworks-punched candle holder, you will also need: red spray paint, white and blue acrylic paint, foam brush, a Miracle Sponge™ (dry compressed sponge available at craft stores), artists' masking tape, paper towels, hammer, large nail or nail punch, flathead screwdriver, and an old towel.
For star-punched candle holder, you will also need: blue spray paint, fabric, masking tape, hammer, large nail or nail punch, an old towel, and a craft glue stick.
For appliquéd candle holders, you will also need: red or blue spray paint, fabric(s), craft glue stick, and a white paint pen and a hot glue gun and glue sticks (optional).

FIREWORKS-PUNCHED CANDLE HOLDER
1. Place can in sink. Screw lid onto empty beverage bottle. Place bottle in can (bottle will allow ice to expand without distorting can). Fill can to rim with water. Place lid on can, securing bottle in can. Freeze can until water is frozen solid.
2. Trace fireworks punching pattern, page 121, onto tracing paper.
3. Arrange pattern on can and use tape to tape in place.
4. Place can pattern side up on towel. Punching through dots on pattern, use hammer and nail to punch holes in can. Use hammer and screwdriver to punch lines at center of design in can. Refreeze can as necessary to keep ice solid.
5. Repeat Steps 3 and 4 as desired (punching pattern can be reused).
6. Run warm water into can to melt ice; remove bottle from can. Dry can completely.
7. Spray paint can red.

8. For stripes on can, use masking tape to mask off about 1¼" at top and bottom of can; use foam brush and liquid acrylic paint to paint masked off areas blue. Remove tape from can.
9. Trace star pattern, shown in gold on page 121, onto tracing paper; cut out. Use pattern to cut star from dry sponge. Dip dampened sponge into white paint; remove excess on a paper towel. Use a stamping motion to paint stars along stripes on can.

STAR-PUNCHED CANDLE HOLDER
1. Use star punching pattern, shown in blue on page 121, and follow Steps 1 - 6 of Fireworks-Punched Candle Holder instructions to prepare can and punch stars in can.
2. Spray paint can blue.
3. Trace star appliqué pattern, shown in blue on page 121, onto tracing paper; cut out. Use pattern to cut same number of stars from fabric as there are stars punched in can. Glue 1 fabric star to center of each punched star.

APPLIQUÉD CANDLE HOLDERS
1. (*Note:* Follow all steps for each candle holder.) Spray paint can red or blue.
2. Trace desired appliqué pattern(s), shown in red on page 121, onto tracing paper; cut out. Use pattern(s) to cut desired appliqué(s) from fabric(s). Use glue stick to glue appliqué(s) to can.
3. If desired, use paint pen to paint dashed lines around appliqués to resemble stitches.
4. If desired, hot glue buttons to can.

*T*his thrifty floorcloth is easy to make using the back of a scrap piece of linoleum. Jaunty jack-o'-lanterns are stenciled onto a striking black and white checkerboard background for this Halloween welcome!

HALLOWEEN FLOORCLOTH

Recycled item: 30" x 60" piece of linoleum.

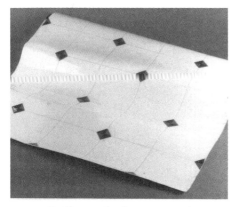

You will also need: white gesso; white, orange, green, brown, and black acrylic paint; large flat and liner paintbrushes; foam brushes; small sponge pieces; matte clear acrylic spray; clear acrylic spray varnish; acetate for stencils; craft knife; cutting mat or folded newspaper; soft cloth; artists' masking tape; yardstick; paper towels; and a permanent felt-tip pen with fine point.

1. (*Note:* Back of linoleum is top of floorcloth.) Use a foam brush to apply 2 coats of gesso to back and edges of linoleum. Paint back and edges of linoleum white.

2. (*Note:* Refer to Diagram for Steps 2 - 6.) Use yardstick and a pencil to draw lines for blocks and borders on linoleum.

3. (*Note:* If necessary, use more than 1 coat of paint.) Using masking tape as necessary to mask off area(s) to be painted, use flat paintbrushes to paint black blocks and orange and green borders on linoleum.

4. For first stencil, cut a piece of acetate 1" larger on all sides than jack-o'-lantern pattern, page 122. Referring to stencil cutting key, page 122, center acetate over pattern and use permanent pen to trace outlines of all areas of first color in key. Repeat for second color in key; for placement guidelines, use dashed lines to outline areas of first color in key.

5. Place each acetate piece on cutting mat and use craft knife to cut out stencil along solid lines, making sure edges are smooth.

6. (*Note:* Follow Step 6 to stencil each jack-o'-lantern on floorcloth.) Hold or tape first stencil in place. Use a clean, dry sponge for each color of paint. Referring to color key, page 122, dip sponge in paint and remove excess on a paper towel (sponge should be almost dry to produce good results). Beginning at edges of cutout area, apply paint in a stamping motion to indicated areas of design. Carefully remove stencil and allow paint to dry. Using second stencil and matching guidelines on stencil to previously stenciled areas, repeat for remaining stencil.

7. Use liner brush to paint white highlights in eyes.

8. Apply 2 coats of matte acrylic spray to floorcloth.

9. To antique floorcloth, mix 1 part brown paint with 1 part water. Working on 1 area at a time, use a clean foam brush to apply mixture to floorcloth; wipe with soft cloth to remove excess. Repeat if darker areas are desired.

10. Apply several coats of varnish to floorcloth. Store floorcloth flat or loosely rolled with painted surface inside.

DIAGRAM

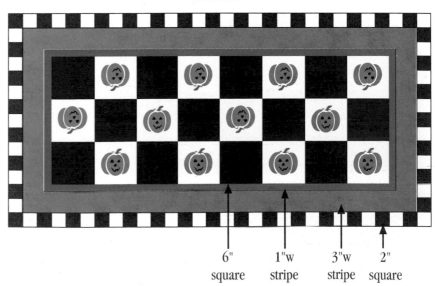

6"
square

1"w
stripe

3"w
stripe

2"
square

HALLOWEEN HANDOUTS

For party favors that little goblins will howl about, try our nifty Halloween treat bags and bottles! Small snack bags are simply turned inside out to reveal a shiny finish, and clear plastic soda bottles make clever containers for candies, trinkets, and other goodies. Miniature balloons and curling ribbon complete the spellbinding containers.

HALLOWEEN TREAT BOTTLES AND BAGS

Recycled items: plastic beverage bottles with lids removed and single serving-size metallic plastic snack bags.

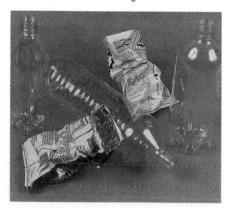

For each bottle, you will also need: a miniature balloon on a stick, curling ribbon to coordinate with balloon, sheer wired ribbon for bow (optional), toys and treats to fill bottle, and a craft knife.
For each bag, you will also need: desired colors of narrow satin ribbon and treats.

BOTTLES

1. (*Note:* Follow all steps for each bottle.) Use craft knife to cut a vertical slit in back of bottle long enough to accommodate items to be placed in bottle. Fill bottle with toys and treats.

2. Tie several lengths of curling ribbon into a bow around neck of bottle. Knot several additional lengths of curling ribbon around neck of bottle. Trim and curl ribbon ends. If desired, tie a length of sheer ribbon into a bow around neck of bottle; trim ends.

3. Place stick of balloon in top of bottle.

BAGS

1. (*Note:* Follow all steps for each bag.) Turn bag inside out and fold top edge about 1" to inside. Fill bag with treats.

2. Tie ribbon lengths into a bow around top of bag; trim ends.

AUTUMN ACCENT

Covered with moss and pinecones, this natural accent is a reminder of fall's bountiful wonders. A spray of dried sunflowers, oak leaves, cedar, and herbs adds color to the rustic wreath.

AUTUMN WREATH

Recycled items: dried oak leaves, small dried sunflowers, and about 13 large pinecones.

You will also need: a 20" dia. wire wreath form, sheet moss, preserved cedar, assorted dried materials (we used tansy, rose veronica, and dried bayberry), a 3" x 4" x 8" floral foam brick, floral picks, greening pins, floral wire, wire cutters, gold acrylic paint, paintbrush, matte clear acrylic spray, and a hot glue gun and glue sticks.

1. Place foam brick at top front of wreath form; wrap with wire to secure. Glue sheet moss over foam brick and wreath form.

2. To attach pinecones to wreath, wrap an 8" length of wire around each end of each pinecone. Beginning and ending at ends of foam brick and alternating direction of pinecones, use wire ends to attach pinecones to wreath; glue if necessary.

3. Paint edges of each leaf with gold paint. With about 2" of pick extending from bottom of leaf, glue a floral pick to back of each leaf.

4. Arrange leaves, sunflowers, cedar, and dried materials in foam brick as desired, using greening pins to secure items in place.

5. Apply acrylic spray to wreath.

THANKSGIVING TABLE RUNNER

*Y*our Thanksgiving table will be appropriately attired when it's dressed up with this timeless table runner. Stamped with shades of autumn using corn shucks, a maple leaf, walnut shells, and wheat stalks, the runner has harvesttime appeal.

THANKSGIVING TABLE RUNNER

Recycled items: assorted natural items for stamps (we used wheat stalks, a maple leaf, walnut shell halves, and corn shucks).

You will also need: fabrics for runner and runner border, paper-backed fusible web, 1/2"w paper-backed fusible web tape, assorted colors of acrylic paint (we used light yellow, dark yellow, gold, light orange, dark orange, rust, dark green, brown, and black), acrylic paint thickener (optional), foam brushes, and a pressing cloth.

1. For runner, cut a fabric piece desired finished size of runner. For border, cut a fabric piece 2¼" larger on all sides than runner fabric piece.

2. Follow manufacturer's instructions to fuse web to wrong side of runner fabric piece. Do not remove paper backing.

3. (*Note:* For stamped designs with more texture, follow paint thickener manufacturer's instructions to thicken paint.) To stamp design on runner fabric, place 1 natural item on a protected work surface and use a foam brush to apply desired color paint to 1 side of item. Press item paint side down onto runner fabric piece. For flexible items, press item onto fabric from center outward. Carefully lift item from fabric. Repeat with remaining items.

4. Cut a 2¼" square from each corner of border fabric piece (Fig. 1).

Fig. 1

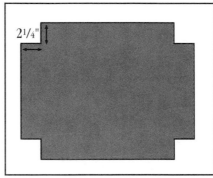

5. Remove paper backing from runner fabric piece. Matching wrong sides, center runner fabric piece on border fabric piece; using pressing cloth, fuse in place.

6. Press 1 side edge of border fabric piece ½" to wrong side. Fuse web tape along pressed edge. Do not remove paper backing. Press edge 1¾" to wrong side, covering edge of runner fabric piece (Fig. 2). Unfold edge and remove paper backing. Refold edge and fuse in place. Repeat for remaining side edge of border fabric piece.

Fig. 2

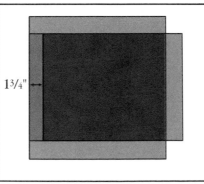

7. Press 1 corner at top of border fabric piece diagonally to wrong side (Fig. 3). Fuse web tape along diagonal edge (Fig. 4); do not remove paper backing. Repeat for remaining corners.

Fig. 3

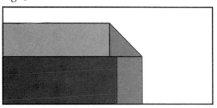

Fig. 4

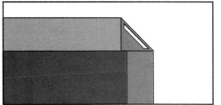

8. Press top edge of border fabric piece ½" to wrong side. Fuse web tape along pressed edge. Do not remove paper backing. Press edge 1¾" to wrong side, covering top edge of runner fabric piece. Unfold edge and remove paper backing from all edges. Refold edge and fuse in place. Repeat for bottom edge of border fabric piece.

FROSTY INSPIRATION

*F*inished with a
sheer bow and a satin
ribbon hanger, this quick
wintry wonder is fashioned
from the lid of a clear plastic
food container. The frosty
snowflake pattern is easily
created by spray painting
over a paper doily.

SNOWFLAKE ORNAMENT

Recycled item: approx. 5¹/₂" square clear
plastic food container (1 container will
make 2 ornaments).

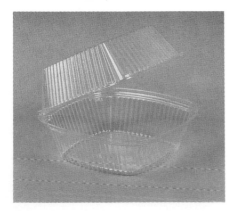

You will also need: a paper doily (at least
4" dia.), 6¹/₂" of ¹/₄"w white satin ribbon,
¹/₃ yd of 1¹/₂"w white sheer wired ribbon,
white floral spray paint, serrated-cut craft
scissors, and a low-temperature hot glue
gun and glue sticks.

1. Use craft scissors to cut top or bottom
from container.

2. Place doily over plastic square and
lightly spray with white spray paint;
carefully remove doily.
3. For hanger, glue ends of satin ribbon
length to 1 corner (top) on front of
ornament.
4. Tie sheer ribbon into a bow; trim ends.
Glue bow over hanger ends.

ELEGANT SNOWBALL

*F*or this lovely ornament, a sock is stuffed with plastic grocery bags and enclosed in a spray-painted mesh produce bag. Gilded trims and a paper rose made from sheet music add a classic touch to the Yuletide pretty.

SNOWBALL ORNAMENT

Recycled items: a white adult-size sock, a mesh produce bag, 5 or 6 plastic grocery bags, and sheet music.

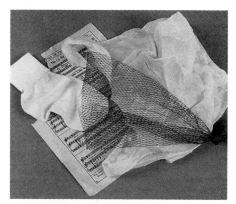

You will also need: 1/2 yd of 1/8" dia. white and gold cord, 1/2 yd of 1/16" dia. gold cord, 5/8 yd of 1"w gold wired ribbon, gold spray paint, artificial berry sprig with greenery, tracing paper, and a hot glue gun and glue sticks.

1. Use sheet music and follow Steps 2 - 4 of Easter Gift Box instructions, page 16, to make 1 rose, cutting a 3" x 4" strip from sheet music for rose center.

2. For ornament, spray paint mesh bag gold. For bottom of ornament, tightly wrap 1 end of gold cord 5 or 6 times around bag about 2" from bottom; glue to secure and trim remaining end. Trim bag about 1 1/2" below cord.

3. Stuff toe of sock with plastic bags to form a ball shape. Place stuffed toe of sock into bottom of mesh bag. Trim sock and bag about 5" from top of ball shape.

4. Fold tops of sock and bag about 4" to inside.

5. For hanger, fold remaining gold cord in half and glue ends inside top of sock.

6. Tie white and gold cord into a bow around bag and sock close to ball shape; knot and trim each end. Glue knot of bow to secure.

7. Glue berry sprig and rose to ornament near cord bow.

8. Tie ribbon into a bow; trim ends. Glue bow to ornament, covering back of rose.

STUNNING CANDLE STANDS

Disguised with paints, berries, and elegant trims, these Christmasy candle holders had humble beginnings. You'd never guess they started with plastic soda bottle tops, empty ribbon spools, and a small cardboard box!

HOLIDAY CANDLE HOLDERS

Recycled items: 2-liter plastic beverage bottles with lids removed, ribbon or trim spools (ours measure 3¼"h and 7¼"h), long narrow cardboard box (box must measure at least 1" square on ends; we used a 1" x 1⁷⁄₈" x 3½" toothpaste box), small pinecones, and small pieces of corrugated cardboard.

You will also need: red and gold artificial berry sprigs, self-adhesive protective rubber pads (if needed), and a hot glue gun and glue sticks.

For each spool candle holder, you will also need: artificial cherries with leaves, gold wire tendrils, wired ribbon (optional), and copper (optional) and gold acrylic spray paint.

For box candle holder, you will also need: ¹⁄₁₆" w gold braid, ³⁄₁₆" dia. gold twisted cord, wired ribbon, aquarium gravel, fleck-style textured spray paint (any color), gold and copper acrylic spray paint, craft knife and cutting mat or folded newspaper, and a permanent felt-tip pen with fine point.

For bottle top candle holder, you will also need: plaster of paris, lightweight handmade paper torn into approx. 1" squares, decoupage glue (either use purchased glue or mix 1 part craft glue with 1 part water to make glue), foam brush, clear acrylic spray varnish, wired ribbon, permanent felt-tip pen with fine point, craft knife, and masking tape.

SPOOL CANDLE HOLDERS

1. (*Note:* Follow all steps for each candle holder.) Spray paint spool and pinecones gold. If desired, lightly spray paint spool copper (we sprayed our large spool candle holder copper).
2. Arrange berry sprigs, cherries, tendrils, and pinecones on spool as desired; glue to secure.
3. If desired, tie a ribbon length into a bow; trim ends. Glue bow to spool.
4. If necessary, adhere rubber pads along edges on bottom of spool to stabilize.

BOX CANDLE HOLDER

1. (*Note:* Use craft knife and cutting mat to cut cardboard.) For candle holder base, draw around 1 end of box twice on cardboard, leaving at least 2" between shapes. Cutting ³⁄₄" outside shape, cut 1 drawn shape from cardboard. Cutting ¹⁄₂" outside shape, cut remaining drawn shape from cardboard; set shape aside. Using large cardboard shape as a pattern, cut a third cardboard piece. Cut drawn shape from center of first large cardboard piece and discard.
2. Glue large cardboard pieces together. Glue 1 end (bottom) of box into opening in first large cardboard piece. Open top end of box. Fill box with aquarium gravel to weight. Glue box lid closed. Center and glue small cardboard piece over top of box.
3. Use permanent pen to draw around a plastic bottle 1³⁄₄" from top. Use craft knife to cut top from bottle along drawn line; discard bottom of bottle. Center bottle top on small cardboard piece; glue in place.
4. Follow manufacturer's instructions to lightly spray candle holder with textured paint.
5. Spray paint candle holder gold. Lightly spray paint candle holder copper.
6. Beginning and ending at back of candle holder, glue braid along edges of top cardboard piece. Repeat to glue braid and cord along edges of bottom cardboard pieces.
7. Arrange berry sprigs on candle holder as desired; glue in place.
8. Tie a ribbon length into a bow; trim ends. Glue bow to candle holder.
9. If necessary, adhere rubber pads to corners on bottom of candle holder to stabilize.

BOTTLE TOP CANDLE HOLDER

1. Use permanent pen to draw around plastic bottle 3½" and 8½" from bottom. Use craft knife to cut along drawn lines. Set bottom of bottle aside; discard middle section.
2. Use masking tape to completely cover opening on inside of bottle top. Place bottle top upside down in bottle bottom. Follow manufacturer's instructions to mix plaster; fill bottle top with plaster and allow to harden. Remove bottle top from bottle bottom. Discard bottle bottom.
3. To cover candle holder, use foam brush to apply decoupage glue to back of 1 torn paper square. Apply paper square to candle holder. Overlapping squares, repeat to cover candle holder completely.
4. Apply varnish to candle holder.
5. Arrange berry sprigs around candle holder; hot glue to secure.
6. Tie a ribbon length into bow; trim ends. Hot glue bow to candle holder.
7. If necessary, adhere rubber pads along edges on bottom of candle holder to stabilize.

*I*t's easy to transform flattened aluminum beverage cans into this cute wintry couple! The perky characters, who seem to be singing at the top of their voices, can be used to add merriment to the tree, accent a wreath, embellish a garland, and much more. They're super inexpensive — and fun to make, too!

CRUSHED CAN COUPLE

Recycled items: one 5.5-ounce and one 12-ounce aluminum beverage can for each snow person and a 1¹⁄₈"h wooden spool and 1³⁄₄" dia. black button for snowman's hat.

You will also need: white spray primer, white spray paint, orange and black acrylic paint, small round paintbrushes, ¹⁄₄" dia. wooden dowel, two ¹⁄₄" dia. black shank buttons with shanks removed for each snow person, artificial snow in a spray can, tracing paper, pencil sharpener, craft saw, and a hot glue gun and glue sticks.

For snowman, you will also need: a 1" x 11" fabric strip for muffler and a 4" square of green felt for mittens.

For snow woman, you will also need: a 6" fabric square cut with pinking shears for shawl, a 4" square of red felt for mittens, small holly sprig with berries, and straw for hair.

SNOWMAN

1. (*Note:* Follow Step 1 for each can. Refer to Fig. 1 for Step 1.) Remove pop-top from can. To bend can, use both hands to hold can with thumbs below top rim and opening toward you. Using thumbs to press on can, bend top rim down. Turn can upside down and repeat for bottom rim, pressing on opposite side of can. Use foot to further flatten can.

Fig. 1

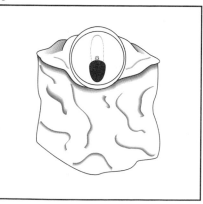

2. Glue small can to top of large can, covering hole in large can.

3. Spray cans with primer, then white paint. For mouth, use a paintbrush to paint inside of can behind opening black; paint black squares on face for eyes.

4. For nose, use pencil sharpener to sharpen 1 end of dowel; paint sharpened end orange. Use saw to cut point from sharpened end of dowel. Glue large end of point to face.

5. Glue ¹⁄₄" dia. buttons to center front of snowman.

6. For mittens, trace pattern, page 122, onto tracing paper; cut out. Use pattern to cut 2 mittens from felt. Glue mittens to snowman.

7. For muffler, fringe ends of fabric strip. Wrap fabric strip around face and tie loosely at 1 side; glue to secure.

8. For hat, paint spool black; glue spool to center of 1³⁄₄" dia. button. Glue hat to head.

9. Lightly spray snowman with artificial snow.

SNOW WOMAN

1. Follow Steps 1 - 6 of Snowman instructions to make snow woman.

2. For hair, glue small pieces of straw to top of head.

3. Glue holly to top of head next to hair.

4. For shawl, fold fabric square in half diagonally. Wrap shawl around head and loosely tie ends at bottom of face; glue to secure.

5. Lightly spray snow woman with artificial snow.

CHRISTMAS GIFT BAGS

*F*rom fast-food restaurant paper sacks to merry gift bags, these Yuletide wrappings are finished in a flash! Once spray painted, the sacks are embellished with Christmas fabrics, ribbon bows, and other festive trimmings.

CHEERY CHRISTMAS BAGS

Recycled items: fast food paper bags.
For snow-flecked bag, you will also need: green spray paint, artificial snow in a spray can, Design Master® Glossy Wood Tone spray, red paper, 1/2 yd of 1/16" dia. gold cord, curling ribbons, 1/4" hole punch, drawing compass, and craft glue.

For "GUESS WHAT?!" bag, you will also need: red spray paint, two 13" lengths of white twisted paper for bag handles, 2 1/4"w metallic ribbon, curling ribbon, white paper, red felt-tip marker with broad point, floral wire, wire cutters, craft glue stick, and a hot glue gun and glue sticks.

For fabric-covered bag with handles, you will also need: red spray paint, fabric, paper-backed fusible web, two 11" lengths of green twisted paper for handles, 22" of 2"w wired ribbon, and a hot glue gun and glue sticks.

For fabric-covered bag with cuff, you will also need: green spray paint, fabric, paper-backed fusible web, curling ribbons, and a 1/4" hole punch.

SNOW-FLECKED BAG

1. Spray paint bag green.
2. Lightly spray bag with artificial snow.
3. For flap, fold top of bag about 2 1/2" to front. For fringe, make 1" long cuts about 1/8" apart into bottom edges of flap.
4. For ornament, use compass to draw two 3" dia. circles on red paper; cut out. Lightly spray 1 side (right side) of each circle with wood tone spray. For ornament hanger, fold a 2" length of cord in half to form a loop. Glue 1/2" of ends of cord to wrong side of 1 circle; glue circles wrong sides together.
5. To attach ornament to bag, punch a hole in 1 side of flap above fringe. Thread remaining cord through loop on ornament and hole in bag; tie ends into a bow about 3" from ornament.
6. Tie 2 lengths of curling ribbon into a bow around cord behind cord bow; curl ribbon ends.

"GUESS WHAT?!" BAG

1. Spray paint bag red.
2. Trace question mark pattern, page 122, onto white paper; cut out. Use red marker to draw stripes on question mark. Use glue stick to glue question mark to bag.
3. For handles, hot glue ends of twisted paper lengths inside top front and back of bag.
4. Follow *Making a Multi-Loop Bow*, page 127, to make a bow without center loop from metallic ribbon. Use lengths of curling ribbon to tie bow to bag handle; curl ribbon ends.

FABRIC-COVERED BAG WITH HANDLES

1. Trim top of bag to desired height. Spray paint bag red.
2. Leaving about 1" between shapes, draw around flattened bag twice on paper side of web. Cutting about 1/2" outside drawn lines, cut out shapes.
3. Follow manufacturer's instructions to fuse web shapes to wrong side of fabric. Cut out fabric shapes just inside lines. Remove paper backing and fuse 1 fabric shape each to front and back of bag.
4. For handles, glue ends of twisted paper lengths inside top front and back of bag.
5. Tie ribbon length into a bow; trim ends. Glue bow to bag.

FABRIC-COVERED BAG WITH CUFF

1. Spray paint bag green.
2. Follow Steps 2 and 3 of Fabric-Covered Bag with Handles instructions to cover front and back of bag with fabric.
3. For cuff, fold top of bag down 1"; repeat.
4. Punch 2 holes about 1" apart at center front of folded part of bag.
5. Thread several lengths of curling ribbon through holes and tie into a bow at front of bag; curl ribbon ends.

Great
GIFTS

Giving great gifts doesn't have to mean spending a fortune, especially when you use our inventive ideas to transform trash into timeless treasures! You'll be delighted by all the wonderful presents — and clever packaging — that you can make from this imaginative collection. There are gifts for everyone, from a secret pal to a sensational spouse. Our luxurious homemade bath oils are ideal for pampering a special someone, and the gardener in the family will love the plant pokes made from pieces of a broken clay flowerpot. For baby, there are cute presents packed in dressed-up plastic soda bottles, and for Grandma, a photo frame fashioned from a detergent scoop. These "recycled" gifts will be admired and appreciated by everyone, especially those concerned with our planet's well-being!

BLUE JEAN BINDERS

Teens are bound to love our terrific scrapbook and photo album! Castaway blue jeans are used to cover an old scrapbook or binder, and waistbands make nifty button closures.

PHOTO ALBUM AND SCRAPBOOK

Recycled items: ring binder or scrapbook, denim jeans, lightweight cardboard, and assorted buttons.

You will also need: a hot glue gun and glue sticks.

For photo album, you will also need: fabric to cover inside of binder, ¹/₂ yd of "ruler" ribbon, white paint pen, and a miniature chalkboard.
For scrapbook, you will also need: fabric, a ³/₄" dia. hook and loop fastener, craft knife, and mementos.

PHOTO ALBUM
1. To cover outside of binder, measure length (top to bottom) and width of open binder. Cut a piece of denim from jeans 2" larger on all sides than binder, piecing as necessary.

2. Center open binder on wrong side of denim piece. Fold corners of denim diagonally over corners of binder; glue in place. Fold edges of denim over edges of binder, trimming denim to fit about 1/4" under binding hardware at top and bottom; glue in place.

3. To cover inside of binder, cut two 2"w denim strips 1" shorter than length (top to bottom) of binder. Press ends 1/4" to wrong side. Center and glue 1 strip along each side of binding hardware with 1 long edge tucked about 1/4" under hardware.

4. Cut 2 pieces of cardboard 1/2" smaller on all sides than front of binder. Cut 2 fabric pieces 1" larger on all sides than 1 cardboard piece. Center 1 cardboard piece on wrong side of 1 fabric piece. Fold corners of fabric diagonally over corners of cardboard; glue in place. Fold edges of fabric over edges of cardboard; glue in place. Repeat to cover remaining cardboard piece.

5. Center and glue covered cardboard pieces inside front and back of binder.

6. (*Note:* Refer to Fig. 1 for Step 6.) For album closure, cut waistband from jeans, leaving top of each belt loop attached to waistband. Center button end of waistband along front opening edge of binder; glue to secure. Continue gluing waistband around binder to center of back of binder; cut waistband close to center back of binder. Remove belt loop closest to cut end of remaining end of waistband and set aside. Close binder. Fasten button of waistband piece on notebook into button hole in loose waistband piece and loosely wrap waistband piece to back of binder. Trim waistband piece to meet raw end of waistband piece on notebook. Glue loose end of waistband piece to back of binder.

Fig. 1

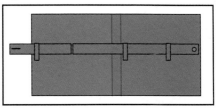

7. Glue detached belt loop over cut ends of waistband. Glue loose end of each remaining belt loop to binder.

8. Use paint pen to write "school days" on chalkboard. Arrange chalkboard and buttons on front of binder; glue in place. Tie ribbon into a bow around 1 belt loop on front of binder; trim ends.

SCRAPBOOK

1. Follow manufacturer's instructions to take scrapbook apart. Lay front and back of scrapbook flat.

2. To cover each scrapbook cover, cut a piece of fabric 1" larger all on all sides than cover. Center cover right side down on wrong side of fabric piece. Fold top and bottom edges of fabric to back of cover and glue to secure. Repeat for side edges.

3. Use craft knife to make a small "X" in fabric over each existing hole in scrapbook covers.

4. Follow manufacturer's instructions to reassemble scrapbook.

5. Follow Steps 4 and 5 of Photo Album instructions to cover inside of front and back of scrapbook.

6. Cut back pockets from jeans. Arrange pockets on scrapbook; glue side and bottom edges of pockets in place.

7. For closure, cut a length from button end of waistband long enough to wrap around opening edges of binder and extend 2" onto front and back covers. Glue 2" of cut end at center of opening edge on back of notebook. Remove 1 belt loop from remainder of waistband and glue loop to notebook over cut edge of waistband (Fig. 2).

Fig. 2

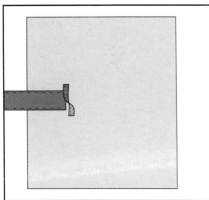

8. Glue 1 part of hook and loop fastener to wrong side of button end of waistband piece. Bring end to front of binder. Glue remaining part of fastener to front of binder to meet first part.

9. Fill pockets with mementos.

DAPPER DESK SET

*D*ad will undoubtedly be delighted to receive these dapper dandies for his desk. Overlapping film negative strips are threaded together using raffia and then taped to fabric-covered cardboard for our smart photo frames. The mosaic look of our catchall box lid is created using eggshell fragments that are tinted with wood-tone spray.

CATCHALL BOX AND FILM FRAMES

Recycled items: eggshells, a small cardboard gift box, 35mm film negatives, large clear plastic food container, cardboard, and glass jar with lid.

For box, you will also need: black and metallic gold spray paint, 1" dia. wooden head bead, matte clear acrylic spray, desired colors Design Master® Wood Tone Spray (we used Glossy and Cherry), household bleach, rubber gloves, paper towels, and craft glue.

For each frame, you will also need: small photograph, fabric to cover frame back and stand, desired color Darice® Straw Satin Radiant Raffia Straw (we used light brown), double-sided tape, spray adhesive, and a hot glue gun and glue sticks.

BOX

1. Remove lid from box. Spray paint box gold. Spray paint box lid and bead black.
2. (*Caution:* Wear rubber gloves and work in a well-ventilated area when working with bleach.) Thoroughly rinse eggshells in water. Place shells in jar and cover with 1 part bleach and 1 part water. Place lid on jar and allow shells to soak at least 24 hours. Remove shells from jar and place on several layers of paper towels to dry.
3. Spray insides and outsides of shells with 2 to 3 coats of wood tone spray(s).
4. Break shells into small pieces. Apply a thick layer of glue to top of box lid. Press shells into glue, covering top of lid.
5. Glue bead to lid for handle. Apply several coats of clear acrylic spray to box and lid.

FRAMES

1. (*Note:* Follow all steps for each frame.) For frame back and photograph cover, determine width and height of area of photograph to be framed; add 2³/4" to each measurement. Cut 1 piece each from cardboard and flat part of food container the determined measurements.
2. To cover frame back, measure width of cardboard and add 2"; measure height of cardboard, add 1", and multiply by 2. Cut a fabric piece the determined measurements.
3. Apply spray adhesive to 1 side of frame back. Place frame back adhesive side down on wrong side of fabric piece and press in place (Fig. 1). Hot glue side edges of fabric to wrong side of frame

back. Hot glue bottom edge of fabric to wrong side of frame back. Hot glue top edge of fabric 1" to wrong side. Hot glue top half of fabric over frame back.

Fig. 1

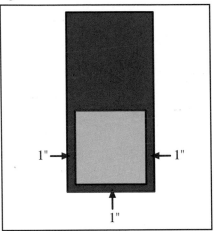

4. For frame front, measure top edge of photograph cover; cut 2 lengths from film negatives the determined measurement. Repeat for 1 side edge of cover.
5. Overlap ends of 1 top and 1 side film length to form 1 corner of frame front. Thread a length of raffia straw through holes in film at corner to form an "X." Knot and trim ends at back. Repeat for remaining corners.
6. Apply lengths of double-sided tape along edges on back of frame front; press frame front onto photograph cover. Apply small pieces of tape to corners on front of photograph; press photograph cover onto photograph. Apply lengths of tape along edges on back of photograph cover. Press photograph cover onto frame back.
7. For frame stand, measure height of frame back; subtract 1". Cut a piece of cardboard 2"w by the determined measurement. Follow Steps 2 and 3 to cover stand. Fold top 1" of frame stand to 1 side (right side). With frame stand centered on back of frame and bottom edges aligned, hot glue area of frame stand above fold to back of frame.

CRAFTY CANDLES

*U*se a little crafting ingenuity to transform old, battered pillar candles into enlightening housewarming gifts! Natural accents such as twigs, berries, dried apples, greenery, sand, and seashells embellish candles that have been coated with melted wax.

NATURALLY CRAFTY CANDLES

Recycled items: pillar or wide round candle for candle base, candle pieces (these are melted and used to attach natural items to candle), crayon pieces to color wax (optional), large cans for melting candle pieces, items to decorate outside of candle (we used sand, shells, twigs, dried apple slices, dried greenery, cranberries, and bay leaves), and a foam food tray at least as long as height of candle (for twig candle only).

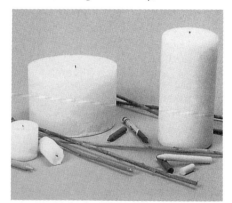

You will also need: either pearl white Candle Magic® wax crystals or paraffin (if needed), a pan to hold cans for melting candle pieces, 1"w craft paintbrushes, and newspaper.

SEASHELL CANDLE
1. Follow *Melting Wax,* page 127, to melt wax to a depth of several inches. Reserve a small amount of prepared wax in a separate can. Add sand to remaining wax until mixture is thick, but still spreadable.
2. Use a paintbrush to apply wax mixture to sides of candle. While wax is still warm, press shells into sides of candle.
3. Use a clean paintbrush to apply a thin coat of reserved wax over each shell; allow to cool completely.

TWIG CANDLE
1. Follow *Melting Wax,* page 127, to melt wax to a depth of several inches.
2. Cut twigs same height as or slightly taller than candle (twigs must fit flat in bottom of food tray).
3. Pour wax into foam tray to a depth of about ¹/₄". Allow wax to cool slightly.

Place twigs in wax side by side with ends even at 1 end (bottom). When wax is cool enough to touch, remove twigs and wax from tray in 1 piece and wrap onto side of candle with even ends of twigs even with bottom of candle. Repeat until candle is covered.
4. Use paintbrush to apply 1 or more coats of wax over candle; allow to cool completely.

APPLE SLICE CANDLE
1. Follow *Melting Wax,* page 127, to melt wax to a depth of several inches.
2. Holding candle at top, dip candle in wax. While wax is still warm, press leaves, greenery, cranberries, and dried apple slices into wax.
3. Use paintbrush to apply 1 or more coats of wax over candle; allow to cool completely.

POTTERY PLANT POKES

*A*n avid gardener will love receiving these savvy plant pokes! Broken pieces of clay pottery are uniquely displayed atop lengths of wire coat hangers that are bent into coils and spray painted to resemble expensive copper wire. Plant names are added to the pokes using a permanent marker.

TERRA-COTTA PLANT POKES

Recycled items: broken terra-cotta pottery and 1 wire coat hanger for each plant poke.

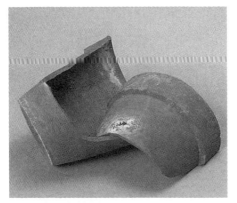

You will also need: spray primer, metallic copper spray paint, black permanent felt-tip pen with medium point, old pillowcase or towel, hammer, pliers, medium-grit sandpaper (if needed), and wire cutters.

1. (*Note:* Handle broken pottery pieces with care.) Place a pottery piece in pillowcase or wrap in towel; use hammer to break piece into desired size smaller pieces. If necessary, sand edges of pottery pieces to smooth.

2. (*Note:* Follow remaining steps for each plant poke.) Use pliers to untwist 1 hanger and straighten hanger wire. Use wire cutters to cut an approx. 25" length from hanger. Use pliers to bend 1 end of wire into a small loop. Bend and curve looped end of wire around pottery piece, securing pottery piece in wire. Bend remainder of wire as desired for stem.

3. Carefully remove pottery piece from wire. Spray wire with primer. Spray paint wire copper. Use black pen to write desired plant name on pottery piece. Replace pottery piece in wire.

4. If necessary, trim stem to desired length.

*F*or gifts that are as good as gold (or silver), give our fashionably eclectic jewelry. You'd never guess that the fabulous fandangles are made from glue and layered brown paper-bag cutouts! The shapes are painted black and then covered with a rub-on metallic finish for an "antique" look. Bead and button accents enhance the handmade earrings and necklaces.

BURNISHED JEWELRY

Recycled items: brown paper bags.
You will also need: rub-on metallic finish (we used gold and silver), black acrylic paint, small paintbrushes, sharp needle, tracing paper, needle-nose pliers to attach jump rings, Aleene's® Tacky Glue, and a craft glue stick.
For silver earrings, you will also need: two 15mm silver leaf beads, 2 dangle earring wires, and 8 silver jump rings.
For silver necklace, you will also need: one 15mm silver leaf bead, other assorted silver beads, black satin cord, 4 silver jump rings, and liquid fray preventative (optional).
For leaf necklace, you will also need: black satin cord, a gold jump ring, and liquid fray preventative (optional).
For bow necklace, you will also need: 1/2" dia. gold shank button with shank removed, black satin cord, dull knife, gold jump ring, liquid fray preventative (optional), and a hot glue gun and glue sticks.

SILVER EARRINGS

1. Cut two 4" squares from a paper bag. Use glue stick to glue squares together.
2. Trace triangle and dangle patterns, page 123, onto tracing paper; cut out. Draw around patterns on square twice. Cut out shapes.
3. Use a paintbrush to apply a thick even coat of Tacky Glue over front of each shape; allow to dry. Repeat for back of each shape.
4. Paint shapes black.
5. Follow manufacturer's instructions to apply metallic finish to shapes, allowing black to show through as desired.
6. Use needle to make 3 holes along bottom edge and 1 hole at top of each triangle and 1 hole at top of each dangle.
7. For each earring, use jump rings to attach dangles to bottom of triangle. Use jump ring to attach 1 leaf bead and top of triangle to earring wire.

SILVER NECKLACE

1. Follow Steps 1 - 6 of Silver Earrings instructions to make 1 triangle with dangles. Use jump rings to attach dangles to bottom of triangle. Attach remaining jump ring to top of triangle and leaf bead.
2. Cut a length of cord about 6" longer than desired finished length of necklace. Thread triangle onto center of cord. Thread 1 bead onto cord at each side of triangle; knot cord close to beads.
3. For each side of necklace, knot cord again about 1" from first knot. Thread additional beads onto cord and knot cord close to last bead.
4. Knot ends of cord together about 2" from ends. Thread a bead onto ends of cord and knot ends together close to bead; trim ends. If desired, apply fray preventative to ends of cord.

LEAF NECKLACE

1. Using leaf pattern, page 123, follow Steps 1 - 3 of Silver Earrings instructions to make 1 leaf.
2. Use Tacky Glue to "draw" veins on 1 side (front) of leaf; allow to dry.
3. Follow Steps 4 and 5 of Silver Earrings instructions to finish shape.
4. Use needle to make a hole at small end of leaf. Attach jump ring to leaf. Cut a length of cord 2" longer than desired finished length of necklace. Thread leaf onto cord. Knot ends of cord together; trim ends. If desired, apply fray preventative to ends of cord.

BOW NECKLACE

1. Using bow pattern, page 123, follow Steps 1 and 2 of Silver Earrings instructions to make 1 bow.
2. Use paintbrush to apply an even coat of Tacky Glue over front of bow. When glue is almost dry, use dull knife to cut texture lines into glue; allow to dry. Apply glue to back of bow and allow to dry. Bend and shape bow as desired.
3. Follow Steps 4 and 5 of Silver Earrings instructions to finish shape.
4. Use needle to make hole at center top of bow. Attach jump ring to bow.
5. Hot glue button to bow.
6. Cut a length of cord 2" longer than desired finished length of necklace. Thread bow onto cord. Knot ends of cord together; trim ends. If desired, apply fray preventative to ends of cord.

SEASHELL SENSATIONS

Like treasures washed ashore by the sea, our powder-room pretties are great pick-me-ups for anyone who needs a little pampering! We created a frame, a potpourri dish, and a jar for holding bath salts or cotton balls — all using seashells collected on summer vacations. Elegant wired ribbon and gilded twisted cord adorn these beautiful accents for the bath.

Recycled items: assorted seashells, approx. 4"h glass jar with lid, and large flat buttons.

You will also need: 1/8" dia. gold and white twisted cord and a low-temperature hot glue gun and glue sticks.

For shell frame, you will also need: a photograph to fit in shell.

For potpourri shell, you will also need: small velvet piece, wide sheer wired ribbon, and potpourri.

For vanity jar, you will also need: small velvet piece, sheer wired ribbon same width as height of jar below lid, 1/4" dia. gold and white twisted cord, fabric marking pencil, pliers, and craft glue.

SHELL FRAME

1. Cut desired area from photograph; glue to inside center of a large shell.

2. Beginning and ending at bottom of photograph, glue cord along edge of photograph.

3. Arrange and glue 3 small shells to large shell below photograph.

4. Cut an approx. 7" length of cord; knot each end. Tie cord into a bow; glue bow at center of small shells.

5. For base, place a button on a flat surface; glue shell frame to button in an upright position.

POTPOURRI SHELL

1. Press a piece of velvet into shell; trim excess velvet along edges of shell. Folding edges about 1/4" to wrong side, glue velvet piece into shell.

2. For base, glue a button to center bottom of shell.

3. Measure outer edge of shell; add 1". Cut a length of ribbon the determined measurement. Fold 1 end of ribbon 1/2" to wrong side. Overlap folded end 1/2" over raw end to form a tube; glue to secure.

4. With seam at back of shell, glue 1 edge of ribbon tube just inside edge of shell.

5. Fill shell with potpourri. Cut an approx. 15" length of cord; knot each end. Gather top of ribbon tube and tie cord into a bow around gathers.

VANITY JAR

1. Measure around widest part of jar; add 1 1/2". Cut a length of ribbon the determined length. Fold 1 end of ribbon 1/2" to wrong side. Overlap folded end 1/2" over raw end to form a tube; hot glue to secure.

2. Place ribbon tube over jar. To gather ribbon at neck of jar, use pliers to grasp wire from unfolded end of ribbon at top of tube. Push ribbon on wire toward folded end until top edge of tube is snug around neck of jar. Fold exposed wire piece to inside of tube, trimming if necessary; distribute gathers evenly and spot glue gathered edge of ribbon to jar.

3. Screw lid onto jar. Mark side of lid at seam in ribbon tube (back of jar); remove lid from jar.

4. Use fabric marking pencil to draw around lid on wrong side of velvet piece. Cut circle from velvet. Use craft glue to glue velvet circle to top of lid.

5. Beginning and ending at mark on lid, hot glue 1/8" dia. cord along edge of velvet circle.

6. Beginning and ending at mark on lid and hot gluing cord in place, wrap 1/4" dia.cord around lid, covering side of lid completely.

7. Hot glue a shell to top of lid.

8. Cut an approx. 20" length of 1/8" dia. cord. Tie cord into a bow around neck of jar; knot and trim each end. Hot glue a small shell over knot at each end of cord.

9. Replace lid on jar.

A Scoopful Of Love

These precious photo frames will make bright gifts for Grandparents Day — or any day you want to share a scoopful of love! To craft one of these cute keepsakes, a picture is glued to a cardboard square, which is affixed to the rim of a sponge-painted plastic detergent scoop. Personalized wired-ribbon bows finish the sweet tokens.

GRANDPARENTS' PHOTO SCOOPS

Recycled items: detergent scoop and cardboard for each scoop.

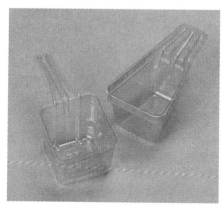

For each scoop, you will also need: photograph, 3 colors of acrylic paint (1 color for basecoat and 2 colors for sponge painting), paint pen to write message on ribbon, dimensional fabric paint to decorate ribbon, 2/3 yd of 1"w wired ribbon, foam brush, small sponge pieces, paper towels, craft glue stick, and a hot glue gun and glue sticks.

1. (*Note:* Follow all steps for each scoop.) Use foam brush to paint scoop with basecoat paint color.

2. To sponge paint scoop, dip a dampened sponge piece into 1 color of paint; remove excess on a paper towel. Using a light stamping motion, use sponge piece to paint scoop. Repeat with a clean sponge and remaining paint color.

3. Place scoop opening side down on cardboard. Draw around scoop (except handle) on cardboard. Use a ruler to draw a line completing top of shape on cardboard. Cutting about 1/8" inside drawn lines, cut out cardboard shape. Trim as necessary to just fit in top of scoop.

4. Center cardboard piece over desired area of photograph to be framed in scoop; draw around cardboard piece on photograph. Cut out photograph along drawn lines. Use stick glue to glue photograph to cardboard piece. Hot glue edges of cardboard piece just inside scoop.

5. Tie ribbon length into a bow around handle of scoop; trim ends. Use paint pen to write desired message on ribbon streamers (we wrote "a scoopful of Love" on 1 streamer and either "for Grandma" or "for Grandpa" on the other).

6. Use dimensional paint to paint flowers, hearts, and dots on streamers as desired.

"PIECE-FUL" WIND CHIME

*O*ur winsome wind chime will welcome one and all as it "sings" in the breeze. Antique silver spoons and broken china pieces wrapped in copper-painted wire are strung from an inverted wicker basket for this artsy home accent. What a wonderful housewarming present!

BITS-AND-PIECES WIND CHIME

Recycled items: small wicker basket without handle, broken china pieces, 5 small silver spoons, and wire coat hangers.

You will also need: spray primer, copper spray paint and spray paint to paint basket, nylon thread, pliers, wire cutters, old pillowcase or towel, hammer, a soft cloth, and craft glue.

1. Spray paint basket desired color.
2. (*Note:* Handle broken china with care.) Place china in pillowcase or wrap in towel; use hammer to break china into small pieces.

3. Use wire cutters to cut 6 approx. 10" wire lengths from hangers. Spray wire lengths with primer. Spray paint wire lengths copper.
4. (*Note:* To protect painted wire while bending, cover wire with soft cloth.) For hanger, use pliers to bend a slight curve in 1 end of 1 wire length. Insert curved end of wire under several reeds at center bottom of basket. Use pliers to bend and curve ends of wire, forming a small loop at end of long end of wire. Thread a 20"

length of nylon thread through loop; knot ends together.
5. For hanger on each china piece, form a small loop at 1 end of another wire length. With loop at top of china piece, bend and curve wire around china piece; trim excess wire if necessary.
6. Alternating spoons and china pieces and spacing items evenly, use varying lengths of nylon thread to tie spoons and china pieces to basket rim. Place a small dot of glue on each knot to secure.

MILK CARTON COTTAGE LAMP

A dd a little whimsy to someone's day by sharing our miniature country cottage light. The home-sweet-home accent is made using a candle lamp and a small painted milk carton.

"HOME-MADE" LAMP

Recycled item: 1-pint cardboard drink carton.

You will also need: 5"h candle lamp; 5¼"h self-adhesive lampshade; fabric to cover shade; an approx. 10" long oval-shaped natural wood plaque; white, pink, red, green, light brown, brown, grey, and dark grey acrylic paint; desired colors of acrylic paint for flowers; assorted paintbrushes; grey spray primer; matte clear acrylic spray; sheet moss; large aquarium gravel to support lamp in carton; white paper; black felt-tip pens with fine and medium points; tracing paper; graphite transfer paper; craft knife; ¾"w masking tape; craft glue; and a hot glue gun and glue sticks.

1. Carefully open top of carton completely.
2. (*Note:* All patterns are on page 123.) Trace cord and lamp opening patterns onto tracing paper; cut out.
3. Center top edge of lamp opening pattern along top edge of 1 side of carton; draw around side and bottom edges of pattern. Use craft knife to cut piece from carton along drawn line. Repeat for opposite side of carton.
4. For "siding," begin at 1 bottom corner and wrap masking tape around carton, ending at top edges of sides of carton.

5. Center fold line of cord opening pattern (shown in grey) along back bottom edge of carton with largest part of pattern on bottom of carton. Draw around pattern. Use craft knife to cut piece from carton along drawn lines.
6. Spray carton with primer. Trace roof pattern onto tracing paper. Use transfer paper to transfer pattern to each side of top of carton.
7. For basecoats, trace black lines of patterns for door, windows, and chimney onto white paper.

8. Paint sides of carton and window framework white, windowpanes and chimney grey, bricks on chimney red, and cat and door brown. Shade roof and windows with dark grey; highlight cat with light brown.

9. For details, trace blue lines of patterns onto tracing paper. Use transfer paper to transfer lines to door and cat. Paint cat's nose pink.

10. Use black pens to draw over all transferred lines and to outline door, windows, and bricks on chimney.

11. Refer to Diagrams, below, for Steps 11 - 13. Cut out door, windows, and chimney. Use craft glue to glue door, windows, and chimney to sides of carton.

12. Use green paint to paint shrubs, vines, trees, and flower stems on house as desired. Use the tip of a paintbrush handle to paint desired color dots at tops of flower stems for flowers and green dots for leaves on vines.

13. Use black pens to outline and add details to shrubs, trees, flowers, roof, and bricks on chimney.

14. Spray carton with several coats of clear acrylic spray.

15. Thread cord of lamp through top of carton and hole at bottom. Insert cord in notch at back of carton. Working inside carton, cover hole in bottom of carton with tape.

16. Hot glue carton to center of plaque.

17. Fill carton with gravel to bottom of roof. Insert bottom end of lamp about 1" into gravel. Pull cord taut. Close top of carton around lamp; hot glue top of carton closed.

18. Use craft glue to glue top of chimney to roof.

19. Hot glue moss to plaque around house as desired.

20. Follow manufacturer's instructions to cover shade with fabric. Place shade on lamp.

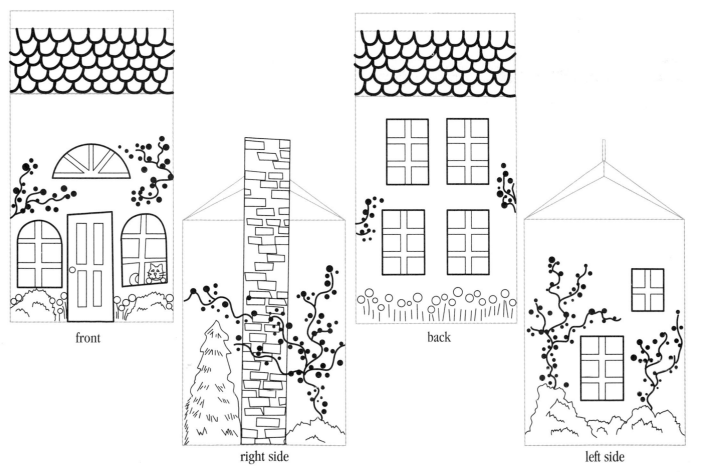

front

right side

back

left side

49

PUZZLING CALENDAR CUT-UPS

*B*affled over what to give a youngster (or someone young at heart)? The solution is simple — everyone loves a good puzzle! Our teddy bear puzzle is crafted from an illustration found in an old calendar. The picture is glued to cardboard, then cut into pieces. To complete the fun set, a container is decorated with a miniature toy and other coordinating trims.

Recycled items: a wall calendar, a piece of cardboard same size as 1 calendar page, and a can with resealable lid to hold puzzle pieces.

For puzzle, you will also need: craft knife, cutting mat or folded newspaper, and spray adhesive.

For can, you will also need: 2 fabrics to cover can and top of lid, lightweight fusible interfacing, small picture cut from back of calendar to match puzzle picture (if available), small toy to match theme of calendar, a short length of narrow wooden dowel, curling ribbon, white and 2 colors of paper, a felt-tip pen, pinking shears, craft glue, and a hot glue gun and glue sticks.

PUZZLE

1. Cut desired page from calendar. Use spray adhesive to glue page to cardboard.
2. Use a pencil to draw shapes for puzzle pieces on back of cardboard (pieces must be small enough to fit in can).
3. Use craft knife and cutting mat to cut out puzzle pieces along drawn lines.

CAN

1. Remove lid from can.
2. Follow manufacturer's instructions to fuse interfacing to wrong sides of fabrics.
3. Measure around can; add 1/2". Measure height of can. Cut a piece of fabric the determined measurements. Overlapping short edges at back, use craft glue to glue fabric to can.
4. Draw around lid on second fabric. Cutting just inside drawn shape, use pinking shears to cut shape from fabric. Use craft glue to glue fabric shape to top of lid.
5. Use craft glue to glue small calendar picture to 1 piece of colored paper. Trim paper to 1/4" from edges of picture. Hot glue picture to front of can.
6. For sign, cut a small piece of white paper. Use pen to write desired greeting on paper piece. Use craft glue to glue white paper piece to second colored paper piece. Trim colored paper to 1/4" from edges of white paper. Hot glue sign to 1 end of dowel.
7. Tie several ribbon lengths into a bow; curl ends.
8. Arrange toy, sign, and bow on lid; hot glue to secure.

LUXURIOUS BATH OILS

*T*hese scented bath oils are a wonderful way to shower a friend with luxury. To create them, empty glass bottles are filled with mineral and essential oils, as well as dried flowers and greenery. The containers are sealed with colored wax and decorated with lace, ribbons, and a charm for a fanciful finish.

BOTTLED BATH OILS

Recycled items: glass bottle with lid or cork, candle pieces (for wax seal on bottle), crayon pieces to color wax (optional), large can for melting candle pieces, and newspaper.

You will also need: mineral oil, desired essential oil (available at health food stores), assorted small dried flowers and greenery, funnel, either pearl white Candle Magic® wax crystals or paraffin (if needed), a pan to hold can for melting candle pieces, items to decorate bottle

(we used lace ribbon, satin and sheer ribbons, gold cord, a gold heart-shaped charm, a heart-shaped lace appliqué, a paper tag with a floral sticker, and a silk rose), and a hot glue gun and glue sticks.

1. (*Note:* If using a bottle with a narrow neck, soak dried flowers and greenery in mineral oil until saturated before placing them in bottle to help prevent breakage.) Place flowers and greenery in bottle. Use funnel to fill bottle with mineral oil. Add about 2 drops of essential oil per ounce of mineral oil. Firmly insert cork into bottle or tightly screw lid on bottle.

2. Follow *Melting Wax*, page 127, to melt wax to a depth of about 1¹/₂".

3. Allowing wax to harden slightly between coats, dip about 1" of top of bottle in melted wax until cork or lid is completely coated.

4. For bottles with lace, measure around bottle; add ¹/₂". Cut a piece of lace the determined measurement. Overlapping ends at back, spot glue lace to bottle.

5. Follow Steps 1 - 3 of *Making a Multi-Loop Bow*, page 127, to make a small bow from desired ribbon. Tie a second length of ribbon around center of bow to secure loops, and use ribbon ends to tie bow to bottle; trim ends.

6. Glue additional decorative items to bottle as desired.

"BUNDLE OF JOY" BOTTLES

F or a special delivery that's sure to delight a mother-to-be, give one of our sweet baby shower gift bundles. Plastic soda bottles are slit and filled with assorted items for newborns, then embellished with ribbons, flowers, and pacifiers.

BABY GIFT BOTTLES

Recycled item: a 2-liter plastic beverage bottle for each gift bottle.

For each bottle, you will also need: small white and desired color silk flowers, white curling ribbon, 1½"w ribbon, pacifier with ring, assorted gift items to fill bottle, craft knife, and a hot glue gun and glue sticks.

1. (*Note:* Follow all steps for each bottle.) Use craft knife to cut a slit in back of bottle long enough to accommodate gifts. Insert gifts into bottle through slit.
2. Tie 1½"w ribbon into a bow around neck of bottle; trim ends.

3. Glue flowers to knot of bow.
4. Knot several lengths of curling ribbon around neck of bottle. Thread half of ribbon ends through ring on pacifier and tie ribbons into a bow; trim and curl ends.

CLEVER CANISTERS

*G*ive teacher a present she's sure to appreciate with our clever gift containers. Painted or covered with fabrics featuring classic classroom designs, cardboard and tin canisters can be filled with lots of sweet treats for a favorite instructor. It's as easy as 1-2-3!

GIFT CANISTERS FOR TEACHERS

Recycled items: lightweight cardboard and cardboard or tin canisters with resealable lids.

You will also need: fabric to cover lid, grosgrain ribbon about the same width as side of lid, either baby rickrack or narrow grosgrain ribbon, low-loft polyester bonded batting, and craft glue.

For fabric-covered canisters, you will also need: fabric, paper-backed fusible web, and card stock paper.

For painted canisters, you will also need: either yellow or black flat spray paint; white, green, red, and brown acrylic paint and small paintbrushes (for "apple" canisters only); 3/4"w "ruler" ribbon (for canister with bow only); tracing paper; and graphite transfer paper.

FABRIC-COVERED CANISTERS

1. Follow manufacturer's instructions to fuse web to wrong side of fabric to cover can. Remove paper backing and fuse fabric to card stock paper.

2. Remove lid from canister and measure height of canister. Measure around sides of canister; add 1/2". Cut a piece of fabric-covered paper the determined measurements.

3. Matching 1 long edge of fabric-covered paper to bottom edge of canister and overlapping short edges at back, glue fabric-covered paper to canister.

4. To cover lid, use a pencil to draw around lid on lightweight cardboard, batting, and wrong side of fabric to cover lid. Cut out cardboard and batting shapes. Cut shape from fabric 1" outside drawn shape. Clip edge of fabric at 1/2" intervals to within 1/8" of shape. Glue batting to cardboard. Center cardboard batting side down on wrong side of fabric. Alternating sides and pulling fabric taut, glue clipped edges of fabric to back of cardboard. Glue covered cardboard to top of lid.

5. For trim on lid, measure around lid; add 1/2". Cut 1 length each from ribbon same width as side of lid and either rickrack or narrow ribbon. Overlapping ends, glue ribbon same width as side of lid around lid. Glue either rickrack or narrow ribbon along center of ribbon on lid.

6. For trim at bottom of canister, repeat Step 5.

PAINTED CANISTERS

1. (*Note:* For canister with "ruler" ribbon, follow Steps 1, 4, and 5 only. Tie ribbon into a bow around canister and trim ends.) Spray paint canister either yellow or black.

2. For canister with row of apples, trace apple pattern, page 124, onto tracing paper. Spacing apples evenly, use transfer paper to transfer design to canister. Paint apples red, stems brown, and leaves green. Paint white highlights on apples and leaves.

3. For canister with apple and numbers, follow Step 2 to transfer and paint 1 apple on canister. Trace number patterns, page 124, onto tracing paper. Use transfer paper to transfer numbers to canister. Paint numbers white.

4. To cover lid, follow Step 4 of Fabric-Covered Canisters instructions.

5. For trim on canister lid and bottom, follow Steps 5 and 6 of Fabric-Covered Canisters instructions.

ROMANTIC WRAPPINGS

*C*reate romantic gift
packaging by embellishing
bubble wrap, a fast food bag,
or an empty food tin with
paints, pressed pansies, and
wrapping paper cutouts.
Coordinating gift tags and
a card complete the
thoughtful lovelies.

BUBBLY GIFT WRAP

Recycled item: bubble wrap.
You will also need: 1 or 2 colors of acrylic spray paint, decorative ribbon, felt-tip pen with fine point, 2 coordinating decorative papers for tag, and a craft glue stick.

1. Trim bubble wrap to desired size.
2. For 1-color wrap, spray paint both sides of wrap desired color.
3. For 2-color wrap, spray flat side of wrap 1 color and lightly spray bubble side of wrap a second color.
4. Center gift on flat side of wrap. Bring edges of wrap up around gift. Adjust gathers in wrap. Tie ribbon into a bow around wrap; trim ends.
5. For tag, use pen to write message on 1 paper piece; cut message from paper. Glue tag to a second paper piece. Cutting 1/8" to 1/4" from edges of tag, cut tag from paper.

PANSY BAG AND CARD

Recycled item: fast food bag.
You will also need: dried pressed flowers and greenery (we used pansies and asparagus fern), clear self-adhesive plastic (Con-tact® paper), and craft glue.
For bag, you will also need: desired color glossy spray paint to coordinate with flowers, several 21" ribbon lengths in assorted widths, two 4" squares of coordinating colored papers for tag, 1/4" hole punch, serrated-cut craft scissors, a black felt-tip pen with fine point, tracing paper, and a hot glue gun and glue sticks.
For card, you will also need: a blank card with envelope, and a gold paint pen with fine point.

BAG

1. Spray paint bag.
2. Place flattened bag on paper side of self-adhesive plastic; draw around bag. Cut out plastic just inside drawn line.
3. Arrange flowers and greenery on flattened bag, leaving about 1 1/2" at top of bag uncovered; use small dots of craft glue to secure flowers and greenery. Remove paper backing from plastic. Align edges of plastic with edges of bag and press in place, sealing flowers and greenery.
4. Place gift in bag. For bow on bag, fold top of bag about 1/2" to front; repeat. Punch 2 holes about 1" apart at center of folded part of bag. Thread ribbon lengths through holes and tie into a bow at front of bag; trim ends.
5. For heart tag, trace pattern, page 124, onto tracing paper; cut out. Use pattern to cut heart from 1 colored paper piece. Use craft glue to glue heart to remaining paper piece. Cutting just outside edges of heart, use craft scissors to cut out heart. Use black pen to draw dashed lines along edge of tag to resemble stitches and write message on tag. Hot glue tag to bow.

CARD

1. Follow Steps 2 and 3 of Bag instructions to apply flowers and greenery to front of card.
2. Use paint pen and a ruler to draw a border about 1/4" inside edges of card.

PANSY TIN

Recycled items: wrapping paper with desired motifs and tin with resealable lid.
You will also need: desired color spray paint, matte clear acrylic spray, ribbon same width as side of lid, ribbon slightly narrower than side of lid, a 1 1/8" square of 1 color of paper and a 1 3/8" x 2 3/4" piece of a second color of paper for tag, black felt-tip pen with fine point, foam brush, soft cloths, decoupage glue (either use purchased glue or mix 1 part craft glue with 1 part water to make glue), and a hot glue gun and glue sticks.

1. Remove lid from tin. Spray paint tin desired color.
2. Follow *Decoupage* instructions, page 127, to decoupage tin.
3. To cover lid, center lid over desired area on wrapping paper; draw around lid. Cut out paper just outside drawn line. Apply decoupage glue to wrong side of paper piece. Press paper piece onto lid and smooth in place, working from center outward.
4. Apply clear acrylic spray to lid.
5. For trim on lid, measure around side of lid; add 1/2". Cut a length from each ribbon the determined measurement. Hot glue wider ribbon to side of lid; center and glue narrower ribbon to wider ribbon.
6. For tag, match short edges and fold large paper piece in half. Use decoupage glue to glue paper square to front of folded paper piece. Use black pen to draw around edges of paper square and write message on tag. Insert corner of tag under edge of lid on tin.

FRAGRANT FIRE STARTERS

*A*n excellent gift for hearth and home, our rustic fire starters are made by filling paper egg cartons with melted candle pieces and dried fruits, spices, or other naturals. The fragrant winter warmers are arranged in a small basket and presented with a handwritten gift tag.

FIRE STARTERS

Recycled items: paper egg carton, candle pieces, crayon pieces to color wax (optional), large can for melting candle pieces, and newspaper.

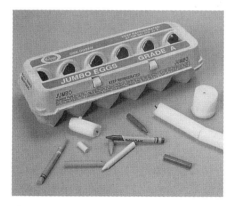

You will also need: a small basket with handle, either pearl white Candle Magic® wax crystals or paraffin (if needed), a pan to hold can for melting candle pieces, assorted dried fruits, cinnamon sticks, spices, greenery, small pinecones, craft ribbon, jute twine, natural excelsior, small fabric and paper pieces for tag, paper-backed fusible web, poster board, craft knife, 6" of floral wire, a black felt-tip pen with fine point, 1/4" hole punch, and a craft glue stick.

1. Follow *Melting Wax,* page 127, to melt wax to a depth of several inches.
2. Use craft knife to cut lid from egg carton.
3. Pour about 1" of wax into each cup of egg carton. Before wax hardens, add desired dried fruits, cinnamon sticks, spices, greenery, or small pinecones to cups. Allow wax to harden completely.
4. Use craft knife to cut each cup from carton just above level of wax.
5. Line basket with excelsior and fill with fire starters.

6. For tag, use black pen to write "for your fireplace!" on paper; cut out. Follow manufacturer's instructions to fuse web to wrong side of fabric piece; remove paper backing. Fuse fabric to poster board. Use glue stick to glue tag to fabric-covered poster board. Cutting about 1/4" from tag, cut tag from fabric-covered poster board. Punch a hole in tag. Thread tag onto twine.
7. Use ribbon and follow *Making a Multi-Loop Bow,* page 127, to make bow. Knot twine on tag around bow and basket handle, securing bow to handle.

LAMPSHADE NIGHT-LIGHTS

Fashioned from clear plastic cups that have been disguised with ribbons and trims, our nifty night-lights look like miniature lampshades. The charming cover-ups can be customized to match any decor.

LAMPSHADE NIGHT-LIGHTS

Recycled items: an approx.
$1^1/2$"w x $1^1/2$"d x $3^1/2$"h night-light and a 9-ounce ($3^3/4$" dia. x $2^3/4$"h) clear plastic cup (1 cup will make 2 night-lights).

You will also need: craft knife and a hot glue gun and glue sticks.
For pleated night-light, you will also need: $1/2$ yd of heavy $4^3/8$"w wired ribbon and 9" of $1/16$"w satin ribbon.
For fringed night-light, you will also need: 7" of $2^3/4$"w wired ribbon and assorted trims.

PLEATED NIGHT-LIGHT

1. For night-light shade, use craft knife to cut cup in half vertically. Discard half of cup or set aside for another night-light. Bottom of cup half is top of night-light shade.

2. Fold each end of wired ribbon length $1/2$" to wrong side and glue in place. Beginning at 1 end, fanfold ribbon into about 1"w pleats. Glue ribbon ends to side edges of shade and adjust pleats; spot glue ribbon to shade as necessary.
3. Tie satin ribbon into a bow; trim ends. Glue bow to shade.
4. Glue top of shade (inside bottom of cup) to top of night-light.

FRINGED NIGHT-LIGHT

1. Follow Step 1 of Pleated Night-light instructions.
2. Wrap ribbon around shade and fold ends to inside (Fig. 1). If necessary, trim ribbon ends to about $1/2$" from side edges of shade. Glue ribbon to shade.

Fig. 1

3. Glue trims along top and bottom edges of shade as desired, folding and gluing ends to inside.
4. Glue top of shade (inside bottom of cup) to top of night-light.

Home Sweet SPRUCE-UPS

A house truly becomes a home when it's given a personal touch by the people who live there. But like many things, tastes and styles change over the years. This crafty collection offers all kinds of ways to dress up or update your decor. Re-using items that would ordinarily be thrown out, you can create anything from a no-sew window treatment to fun, folksy furnishings — all without breaking your pocketbook! You'll discover elegant accents such as lush tassels and decorative fabric-covered books, as well as practical pretties, including the wallpaper-covered dresser shown here. So when your abode is in need of some added flair or a refreshing pick-me-up, look to Home Sweet Spruce-Ups!

NO-SEW PILLOWS

Wrapped in playful animal prints, these no-sew throw pillows will add character to your couch! Worn-out pillows are given a face-lift in a matter of minutes using fabrics and basic crafting skills.

Recycled items: pillows.
You will also need: fabrics to cover pillows, safety pins, and fabric glue.
For pleated pillow, you will also need: an oversize button and thread to match button.

PLEATED PILLOW

1. Measure width of pillow; multiply by 2 and add 4". Measure height of pillow; multiply by 2.5 and round down to the nearest whole number. Cut a piece of fabric the determined measurements.
2. Press 1 long edge of fabric 1" to wrong side; glue to secure.
3. Position fabric wrong side up with long edges at sides. Center pillow on fabric. Overlap pressed long edge of fabric over unpressed long edge at center of pillow; glue to secure.
4. For top flap, refer to Fig. 1 to fold top end of fabric over pillow. Repeat to fold bottom end of fabric for bottom flap; fold raw edge of bottom flap to wrong side so fold is at center of pillow. Concealing safety pins in fabric, use safety pins to secure flaps in place.

Fig. 1

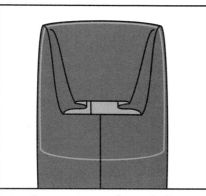

5. Sew button to center front of pillow over flaps.

KNOTTED PILLOW

1. Measure width of pillow; multiply by 4. Measure height of pillow; multiply by 2 and add 4". Cut a piece of fabric the determined measurements.
2. Press 1 long edge of fabric 1" to wrong side; glue to secure.
3. Position fabric wrong side up with long edges at top and bottom. Center pillow on fabric. Overlap pressed long edge of fabric over unpressed long edge at center of pillow; glue to secure.
4. Knot ends of fabric at center of pillow. Fold ends of fabric to wrong side of knot, concealing raw edges; use safety pins to secure.

TABLETOP MOSAICS

*P*erfect furniture for the porch or sunroom, old wrought-iron furnishings are dressed up with stunning mosaic tabletops using broken pieces of china and ceramic tiles. We chose two creative designs — one crafted in a classic blue and white color scheme and the other with a bold sunflower motif.

BROKEN-CHINA TABLES

Recycled items: a wrought-iron table and broken china pieces for each table.

You will also need: paintbrushes and desired color(s) of acrylic paint to paint table (optional), ceramic tiles to coordinate with china pieces for edges of design (we used about fifteen 2¹/₄" square tiles for the edges of our 14" x 24" tabletop and about ten 2¹/₄" square tiles for the edges and background of our 9" square tabletop), desired color tile grout

(we used white), tile cutter and tile sander (if needed), ¼" plywood and saw (for tabletop base; if needed), glass cut to cover tabletop and rubber spacers (optional), hammer, either sandpaper or steel wool and tack cloth (if needed), old pillowcase or towel, silicone spray (if needed), and thick craft glue.

1. If painting table, prepare table for painting by lightly sanding table or rubbing with steel wool to smooth any rough areas or to roughen slick surfaces for better paint adhesion; use tack cloth to remove dust. Paint table as desired.
2. (*Note:* If covering existing tabletop, remove tabletop from table and begin with Step 3. To cut plywood for tabletop base, begin with Step 2. If you do not have access to a circular saw or table saw, many home centers will cut plywood to size on a cost-per-cut basis.) If necessary, remove existing tabletop from table. Measure width and length of top of table, measuring inside lip that holds tabletop. Subtract ⅛" from each measurement. Cut a piece of plywood the determined measurements. Lightly sand edges of plywood. Use tack cloth to remove dust.
3. (*Note:* Handle broken tile and china pieces with care. If necessary, use tile cutter to cut pieces to fit and tile sander to sand sharp edges. If finished tabletop will not be covered with glass, keep tile and china pieces as level as possible.) For tile edges on tabletop, place tiles in pillowcase or wrap in towel; use hammer to break tiles into large pieces, retaining as many straight edges of tiles as possible for edges of table.
4. Arrange tile pieces along edges of tabletop with straight unbroken edges of tile pieces along outer edges of tabletop.
5. For design on tabletop, place china pieces in pillowcase or wrap in towel; use hammer to break china into desired size

pieces. Arrange pieces on tabletop as desired. Use either tile or china pieces to fill in background around design.
6. Glue tile and china pieces to tabletop to secure. Allow to dry.
7. Follow manufacturer's instructions to apply grout between china and tile pieces on tabletop.

8. Place tabletop on table. If table will be used outdoors, spray table with silicone spray.
9. If desired, place glass over tabletop, using rubber spacers as necessary to protect glass and keep glass level.

COUNTRY GARDEN MIRROR

Reflecting the charm of a country garden, our enchanting mirror is bordered with a latticework of twigs and silk ivy. Floral fabric cutouts embellished with grapevine hearts provide a feminine touch for this lovely piece.

COUNTRY GARDEN MIRROR

Recycled items: rectangular mirror with hanger (our mirror measures 24" x 28") and straight twigs.

You will also need: 1/4" foam core board for frame, spray paint, Design Master® Glossy Wood Tone spray, 4 small heart-shaped grapevine wreaths, fabric for inserts in hearts, paper-backed fusible web, poster board, latex ivy vine, utility knife, cutting mat or folded newspaper, and a hot glue gun and glue sticks.

1. For frame, determine size of area of mirror to be framed (we left a 16" x 20" area of our mirror uncovered); use a pencil and ruler to draw a rectangle the determined size at center of foam core board. Determine desired width of frame and draw a second rectangle the determined distance outside first rectangle (outer dimensions of frame must be at least as large as mirror). Use utility knife and cutting mat to carefully cut frame from foam core board along drawn lines, making sure edges are smooth.

2. Spray paint 1 side (front) and edges of frame. Lightly spray frame with wood tone spray.

3. Center and glue frame to front of mirror.

4. For fabric inserts in heart wreaths, follow manufacturer's instructions to fuse web to wrong side of fabric. Remove paper backing. Fuse fabric to poster board. Draw around outer edges of each wreath on fabric-covered poster board. Cut out hearts about 1/4" inside drawn lines. Glue fabric hearts to backs of wreaths.

5. Glue wreaths to corners of frame. Using utility knife to cut twigs to varying lengths, glue twigs along outer and inner edges of frame. Arrange and glue smaller twigs to frame as desired (we glued our smaller twigs in a zigzag pattern). Arrange and glue ivy to frame as desired.

KOOKY COOKIE KEEPER

*T*o create this colorful cookie jar, we simply decorated a clear glass container with rickrack, vibrant wooden beads, and whimsical animal crackers. It'll be hard to keep little hands out of this cute cookie keeper!

ANIMAL CRACKER COOKIE JAR

Recycled item: large wide-mouth glass jar with lid.

You will also need: animal crackers (we used 5), 1¼" dia. wooden knob with screw, assorted wooden beads, rickrack, ¹/₁₆"w satin ribbon, spray primer, spray paint, clear pour-on epoxy finish (available in 4-ounce kits at craft stores), craft drill, screwdriver, and a hot glue gun and glue sticks.

1. Drill a hole in center of jar lid to fit knob screw. Attach knob to lid.
2. Spray paint knob and lid. Glue additional beads to lid as desired.
3. Glue rickrack to sides of jar and lid as desired.
4. Follow manufacturer's instructions to apply epoxy finish to desired number of crackers, completely covering front and back of each cracker.
5. Measure around jar; add 10". Cut a length of ribbon the determined measurement. Thread beads onto ribbon in groups, leaving enough space for crackers between groups. Knot ribbon around jar; trim ends.
6. Separate beads on ribbon into groups; glue crackers to ribbon and jar, gluing 1 cracker over knot in ribbon.

THRIFTY TABLE SETTING

It's easy to create a designer place setting using wallpaper scraps to match your kitchen or dining room decor! We used vinyl-coated remnants for a wipe-clean place mat, and teapot motifs cut from coordinating borders decorate a clear glass plate and napkin ring. Fashioned from a machine-hemmed fabric square, a floral napkin completes the cozy ensemble.

TABLE SETTING

Recycled items: vinyl-coated wallpapers with desired motifs, heavy cardboard, and a cardboard tube for napkin rings (we used a paper towel tube; 1 tube will make several napkin rings).

You will also need: a clear glass plate, an 18$^{1/2}$" fabric square for napkin, thread to match fabric, heavy duty paper-backed fusible web, tracing paper, white poster board, foam brush, small sharp scissors, matte clear acrylic spray, a pressing cloth, and craft glue.

PLACE MAT

1. Cut a 14" x 17" piece from heavy cardboard. Cut a 20" x 23" piece from 1 style of wallpaper for back and borders of place mat. Cut a 9" x 12" piece from a second style of wallpaper for place mat front.

2. Follow manufacturer's instructions to fuse web to wrong sides of wallpaper pieces. Remove paper backing.

3. Refer to Fig. 1 to cut a 3" square from each corner of large wallpaper piece.

Fig. 1

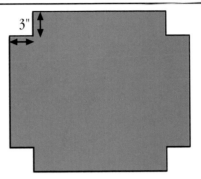

4. (*Note:* Use pressing cloth when fusing.) Center cardboard on wrong side of large wallpaper piece. Fold top and bottom edges of wallpaper over edges of cardboard and fuse in place.

5. Fold corners of side edges diagonally; unfold corners and cut along fold lines (Fig. 2). Fold side edges to front of cardboard; fuse in place.

Fig. 2

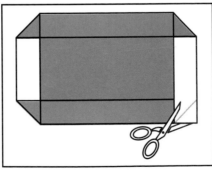

6. Center and fuse small wallpaper piece to front of place mat. Turn place mat over and fuse wallpaper on back of place mat in place.

DECOUPAGED PLATE

Note: To preserve decoration, plate should be wiped clean with a damp cloth after use.

1. Place plate bottom side up. For pattern, trace shape of center of plate onto tracing paper; cut out. Center pattern over desired area of wallpaper and use a pencil to lightly draw around pattern; repeat. Cut out shapes along drawn lines.

2. For decoupage glue, mix 1 part craft glue with 1 part water. Use foam brush to evenly apply glue to center bottom of plate. With right side of wallpaper piece facing plate, place 1 wallpaper piece on plate and smooth in place, working from center outward and gently smoothing any wrinkles or bubbles with brush. Glue wrong side of remaining wallpaper piece to bottom of plate.

3. Allowing to dry after each coat, apply 2 to 3 coats of decoupage glue to bottom of plate, covering edges of wallpaper pieces.

NAPKIN AND NAPKIN RING

1. For napkin, press edges of fabric $^{1/4}$" to wrong side; press $^{1/4}$" to wrong side again and stitch in place.

2. For napkin ring, cut a 1$^{3/4}$" long piece from cardboard tube. Measure around tube and add $^{1/2}$". Cut a strip of wallpaper at least 2"w by the determined measurement. If desired, use small scissors to trim along long edges of wallpaper strip for decorative edging. Center and glue wallpaper strip around tube.

3. Cutting about $^{1/4}$" outside motif, use small scissors to cut desired motif from wallpaper to fit on napkin ring. Glue cutout to poster board. Cutting along edges of motif, cut out motif. Apply 2 to 3 coats of acrylic spray to motif. Glue motif to napkin ring at seam.

4. Fold napkin as desired; insert napkin into napkin ring.

WINDOW FANCIES

*A*dd a welcoming touch to your decor with our fancy floral window treatment. A length of print fabric is elegantly draped over a fabric-covered cardboard tube. For a sweet finale, the poufs are simply tied in place.

Recycled items: 60" long cardboard tube from a fabric bolt for rod (we found our tube at a fabric shop), two 12-ounce can plastic 6-pack holders, and plastic grocery bags.

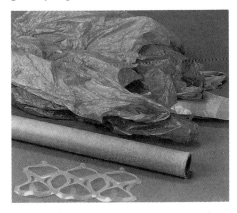

You will also need: fabric to cover rod and finials, 45"w fabric for swag and poufs (we used about 4 yds for our swag and 1 yd for each pouf), mounting brackets to hold cardboard tube, polyester bonded batting, 1/2"w paper-backed fusible web tape, chenille stems, utility knife, tape measure, safety pins, and a hot glue gun and glue sticks.

Note: Window treatment will fit windows up to 48"w.

1. Determine location of poufs for window treatment. Mount brackets at determined locations on wall.
2. For rod, measure distance between brackets; add 12". Use utility knife to cut cardboard tube the determined length.
3. To cover rod, cut a 12"w fabric strip same length as tube.
4. To hem fabric strip, follow manufacturer's instructions to fuse web tape along 1 long edge on wrong side of fabric strip. Do not remove paper backing. Press edge to wrong side along inner edge of tape. Unfold edge and remove paper backing. Refold edge and fuse in place.

5. Glue fabric strip around tube, overlapping hemmed edge over unhemmed edge.
6. (*Note:* Follow Steps 6 - 8 for each finial.) For finial, place 1 plastic bag over 1 end of rod. Stuff bag with additional bags to form desired size ball. Secure outer bag to end of rod with a chenille stem. Trim edges of bag to about 1" from chenille stem. Measure around finial (Fig. 1). Cut a circle of batting the determined measurement. Add 8" to determined measurement and cut a circle from fabric.

Fig. 1

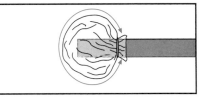

7. Wrap batting around finial; glue in place. Center fabric circle over finial and gather edges around rod; adjust gathers evenly and tightly wrap a chenille stem around fabric and rod close to finial. Wrap another chenille stem around fabric and rod close to edges of fabric.
8. To cover chenille stem closest to each finial, measure around rod at chenille stem; add 1". Cut a 1 1/2"w strip of fabric the determined measurement. Fuse web tape along 1 long edge on wrong side of fabric strip. Do not remove paper backing. Press remaining long edge of fabric to wrong side to meet closest edge of tape. Press taped edge to wrong side along inner edge of tape. Unfold edge and remove paper backing. Refold edge and fuse in place. Glue trim over chenille stem on rod, overlapping ends at back.
9. Mount rod in brackets.
10. To determine length of swag, drape tape measure from top of rod at 1 bracket

to top of rod at remaining bracket. Adjust tape measure to desired length of lower edge of swag and record measurement. To determine length of each cascade at each side of swag, hang tape measure from 1 bracket, adjusting tape measure to desired length; multiply by 2 and record. Add measurements together; add 1" for hems. Cut fabric from selvage to selvage the determined length.
11. Follow Step 4 to hem short, then long edges of fabric piece.
12. Center and drape fabric over rod as desired, covering raw edges of fabric on rod. Use safety pins to secure fabric in place.
13. (*Note:* Follow Steps 13 and 14 for each pouf.) Cut a 1 yd fabric piece from selvage to selvage. Fold one-third of a 6-pack holder to 1 side and use a chenille stem to secure (Fig. 2).

Fig. 2

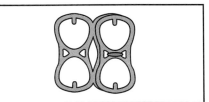

14. Place pouf fabric right side up with folded 6-pack holder at center. Beginning at center of folded holder, pull sections of fabric through rings of holder as shown in Fig. 3, adjusting poufs to desired fullness. Adjust fabric to cover plastic holder, gluing if necessary to secure. Use a chenille stem to attach pouf to rod over 1 bracket.

Fig. 3

GOOD-AS-GOLD FRAMES

*P*lain picture frames can be transformed into opulent accents using gold dimensional and acrylic paints. Garage sales and flea markets are great places to find old, unwanted frames that are ideal for this project.

GILDED DIMENSIONAL FRAMES

Recycled items: picture frames.

You will also need: gold dimensional paint, Duncan® Precious Metals solid gold acrylic paint, and a foam brush.

1. Use dimensional paint to paint dots and lines as desired on frames for texture.
2. Use foam brush to paint frame with acrylic paint.

An Illuminating Idea

An illuminating addition to any room, our stylish tabletop lamp is crafted from a tin juice can embellished with gold cord. A starry fabric-covered shade completes this glimmering creation.

SILVER-AND-GOLD LAMP

Recycled item: 46-ounce juice can with top removed and a 4⁵/₈" dia. wooden frame.

You will also need: a lamp kit for wood or ceramic base, plastic grommet to fit around cord in lamp kit, self-adhesive shade to fit lamp, fabric to cover shade, 1/8" dia. gold twisted cord, gold spray paint, gold craft foil and foil adhesive, glossy clear acrylic spray, 1/4" foam core board, craft knife, hand drill, spring-type clothespins, craft glue, and a hot glue gun and glue sticks.

1. For lamp base, spray paint frame gold. Follow manufacturer's instructions to apply craft foil to frame. Apply acrylic spray to frame.

2. (*Note:* Bottom of can is top of lamp.) To strengthen bottom of can, draw around 1 end of can on foam core board. Use craft knife to cut out circle just inside drawn line. Hot glue circle into bottom of can.

3. Turn can upside down. Follow lamp kit manufacturer's instructions to drill a hole at center bottom of can (top of lamp). Drill a second hole at back of can about 1/4" from open end to fit grommet.

4. Follow lamp kit manufacturer's instructions to assemble lamp, placing grommet on cord and securing grommet in hole at back of can.

5. Center open end of can on front of frame; hot glue in place.

6. (*Note:* To prevent cord from fraying, apply craft glue to 1/2" of cord around area to be cut before cutting cord.) Hot glue lengths of gold cord around can as desired. For top of lamp, begin at center and coil cord around lamp hardware; continue coiling cord to edge of can, gluing cord in place and trimming to fit.

7. Follow manufacturer's instructions to cover shade with fabric.

8. For trim at top of shade, measure around top edge of shade. Cut 2 lengths of cord the determined measurement. Beginning at shade seamline, use craft glue to glue cord lengths along top edge of shade. Use clothespins to secure cord until glue is dry. Repeat for trim at bottom of shade.

73

*O*ld hardbound books
are used to create these
exquisite tabletop treasures.
For a decorative book stack,
several tattered volumes are
covered with rich fabrics
and embellished with wired
ribbon, gilded trims, and
brass charms. An open book
is adorned with a small
picture frame and displayed
on an easel for another
cherished token.

DECORATIVE BOOK STACK

Recycled items: hardbound books.
You will also need: fabrics, 1¹⁄₂"w and
3"w wired ribbons, gold flat trims
(optional), brass charms, and a hot glue
gun and glue sticks.

1. To cover each book with fabric, place
open book on wrong side of fabric. Cut
fabric 1¹⁄₂" larger on all sides than book;
cut notches in fabric at top and bottom of
book spine (Fig. 1). Fold corners of
fabric diagonally over corners of cover;
glue to secure. Fold edges of fabric over
edges of cover; glue to secure.

Fig. 1

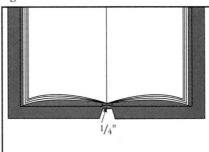

2. If trim on spine or cover is desired, cut
a length of trim ¹⁄₂" longer than spine or
cover. Center and glue trim to spine or
cover; fold ends to inside of spine or
cover and glue in place, trimming if
necessary.
3. Stack books and tie a 3"w ribbon
length into a bow around book(s) as
desired; trim ends. Glue gold trims to
ribbon as desired.
4. For decorative ribbon loop, form a
length of 1¹⁄₂"w ribbon into a loop,
twisting ribbon to secure; trim ends. Glue
charms to loop at twist. Glue loop to
books.

PICTURE FRAME BOOK

Recycled item: a hardbound book.
You will also need: 1¹⁄₂"w and 3"w wired
ribbons, wooden book easel, acrylic spray
paint, brass frame charm (ours measures
2³⁄₈" x 3¹⁄₄"), a photograph to fit in
charm, additional brass charms, and a
hot glue gun and glue sticks.

1. Open book to center. Measure book
from top to bottom; multiply by 2 and
add 2". Cut 2 lengths of 3"w ribbon and 1
length of 1¹⁄₂"w ribbon the determined
measurement. Finger press 1 end of each
ribbon length ¹⁄₂" to wrong side.
Overlapping pressed end over unpressed
end at back, center and wrap one 3"w
ribbon length around right side of open
book; glue to secure. Repeat with 1¹⁄₂"w
ribbon, centering narrow ribbon on wide
ribbon. Repeat to glue remaining ribbon
length loosely around left side of book.
2. Glue photograph in frame charm.
Pinch ribbon on left side of book at
center to gather. Glue frame charm over
gathered ribbon.
3. For decorative ribbon loop, form a
length of 3"w ribbon into a loop, twisting
ribbon to secure; trim ends. Glue charms
to loop at twist. Glue loop to book.
4. Spray paint book easel. Place book on
easel.

"RECYCLED" DESK ORGANIZERS

THREE-PIECE DESK SET

These dandy desk accessories look like they came from an expensive department store, but the clever ensemble is actually crafted from throw-away containers. Covered in pick-me-up plaid fabric, our handy set includes a pencil cup, a stamp roll holder, and a card caddy.

Recycled items: approx. 4.5-ounce and 15.5-ounce cans, approx. 23-ounce detergent box, and canceled stamps.

You will also need: fabric, Darice® Straw-Satin Radiant Raffia Straw, clear nylon thread, small pencil, small envelope, 1/8" hole punch, and a hot glue gun and glue sticks.

PENCIL HOLDER
1. Measure around large can and add 1"; measure height of can and add 3". Cut a piece of fabric the determined measurements.
2. Press 1 long edge and 1 short edge of fabric 1/2" to wrong side. With long pressed edge even with bottom of can, glue fabric around can, overlapping pressed short edge over unpressed short edge. Glue excess fabric to inside of can. Tie a length of raffia straw around can, tie ends into a bow around small pencil, and tie ends into a second bow; trim ends.

STAMP ROLL HOLDER
1. Measure around small can and add 1"; measure height of can and add 1". Cut a piece of fabric the determined measurements. For top of can, measure diameter of can and add 1"; cut 2 fabric squares the determined measurement.
2. Matching wrong sides, press 1 fabric square in half. Center fold of square across center of can opening; glue raw edges of square to sides of can. Repeat to cover remaining half of can opening, using remaining fabric square and matching folds at center of can.
3. Press each long edge and 1 short edge of remaining fabric piece 1/2" to wrong side. Glue fabric around can, overlapping pressed short edge over unpressed short edge.
4. Use small dots of glue to secure stamps to stamp holder. Tie a length of raffia straw into a double bow around holder; trim ends.

CARD HOLDER
1. Remove lid of detergent box. Measure around box; add 1". Measure height of box; multiply by 2 and add 1/2". Cut a piece of fabric the determined measurements.
2. Press 1 long edge and 1 short edge of fabric piece 1/2" to wrong side. With long pressed edge even with bottom of box, glue fabric around box, overlapping pressed short edge over unpressed short edge. Glue excess fabric to inside of box.
3. Tie a length of raffia straw into a double bow around box; trim ends. Punch a hole in 1 top corner of envelope. Use a length of nylon thread to tie envelope to raffia straw on box.

CHARMING CHAIR

To transform a corner into a cozy niche, use this handy idea to convert an orphaned chair into a one-of-a-kind accent! An old chair in need of refinishing is given a quick fix using paints in springtime colors. A simple floral motif from the new fabric-covered seat cushion is used to create a stencil for the painted flowers.

CHARMING CHAIR

Recycled item: wooden chair with removable padded seat.

You will also need: fabric to cover seat, foam rubber to replace seat cushion (if needed), desired colors of acrylic paint to coordinate with fabric, stencil brushes and other assorted paintbrushes, acetate for stencils, fine sandpaper or steel wool, tack cloth, spray primer, matte clear acrylic spray, craft knife, cutting mat or folded newspaper, utility knife, staple gun, permanent felt-tip pen with fine point, paper towels, and removable tape (optional).

1. Remove seat from chair.
2. To prepare chair for painting, lightly sand or rub steel wool over chair to smooth any rough areas or to roughen slick surfaces for better paint adhesion; use tack cloth to remove dust.
3. Apply primer to chair. Paint desired color basecoat(s) on chair (we painted bands of color on legs).
4. (*Note:* For the flower designs on our chair, we chose simple flower and leaf motifs from our fabric to make stencils. Follow Steps 4 and 5 to make stencils and paint designs on chair.) For each stencil, cut a piece of acetate at least 1" larger on all sides than selected fabric motif. Center acetate over motif. Use permanent pen to trace motif onto acetate. For motifs with more than 1 part (for example, a flower with a flower center), make stencil for larger part before making stencil for smaller part. On stencil for smaller part, use dashed lines to trace remaining parts of motif onto acetate to use for guidelines when positioning stencil. Use craft knife and cutting mat to cut out each stencil along solid lines, making sure edges are smooth.
5. To stencil design, either hold or tape first stencil in place. Use a clean dry stencil brush for each color of paint. Dip brush in paint and remove excess paint on a paper towel. Brush should be almost dry to produce good results. Beginning at edges of cutout area, apply paint in a stamping motion. If desired, shade design by stamping additional paint around edges of cutout area. Carefully remove stencil. Repeat as desired. Repeat with remaining stencils.
6. Paint additional accents on chair (we painted stripes along chair back, seat, and lower braces of chair and outlined stenciled motifs and elements of chair back).
7. Spray chair with 2 to 3 coats of clear acrylic spray.
8. (*Note:* If replacing foam rubber on seat, follow Steps 8 and 9. If covering old padding, follow Step 9.) Remove old padding from seat and discard. Use permanent pen to draw around seat on new foam. Use utility knife to cut shape from foam along drawn lines.
9. To cover seat, cut a piece of fabric large enough to wrap around foam and seat and overlap 2" onto bottom of seat on each side. Center foam shape, then seat upside down on wrong side of fabric piece. Folding fabric gift-wrap style at front, alternating sides, and pulling fabric taut, staple edges of fabric to bottom of seat, trimming excess fabric as necessary. Reattach seat to chair.

*O*ur quick fabric wrap makes it easy to dress up old accent pillows to match your decor or to cover small stains. The poufy "bow" is created by threading the ends of the fabric through plastic rings from a 6-pack of soft drinks. The raw edges of the fabric are tucked under and glued in place.

Recycled items: pillow and one 12-ounce can plastic 6-pack holder.

You will also need: fabric to wrap pillow, 1/2"w paper-backed fusible web tape, chenille stem, and a hot glue gun and glue sticks.

1. Measure width of pillow; multiply by 3.5. Measure height of pillow; multiply by 2. Cut a piece of fabric the determined measurements.

2. Follow manufacturer's instructions to fuse web tape along 1 long edge on right side of fabric. Remove paper backing. Matching right sides and long edges, fuse long edges together to form a tube. Turn tube right side out. With seam along 1 long edge, lightly press fabric tube.

3. Fold 6-pack holder into thirds and secure with chenille stem (Fig. 1).

Fig. 1

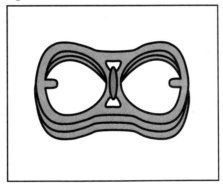

4. Center pillow on fabric tube.

5. Fold ends of fabric toward center of pillow and insert 1 end into each opening of folded 6-pack holder. Distributing gathers evenly to form each side of pouf, tuck ends of fabric back up through holder (Fig. 2).

Fig. 2

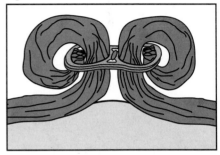

6. Adjust fabric on each side of pouf to cover 6-pack holder; glue fabric in place.

SHOE-BOX FLOWER BASKET

PANSY CENTERPIECE

Silk pansies and greenery add springtime appeal to this sunny centerpiece! The blooms are nestled in a bed of moss, which covers an old shoe box filled with floral foam. To create the look of an ornate wire basket, the arrangement is wrapped with painted plastic 6-pack rings and given a handle made from a coat hanger and crumpled brown paper.

Recycled items: 12-ounce can plastic 6-pack holders (we used 5 holders to fit around an average-size shoe box), shoe box without lid, wire coat hanger, wire pants hanger with cardboard tube, and a brown paper bag.

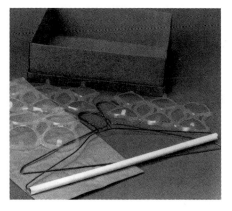

You will also need: sphagnum moss, sheet moss, silk grass and pansies with leaves, floral foam to fit in shoe box, black acrylic spray paint, floral wire, wire cutters, utility knife, foam brush, craft glue, and a hot glue gun and glue sticks.

1. Use lengths of floral wire to attach 6-pack holders together at ends to form a chain (Fig. 1).

Fig. 1

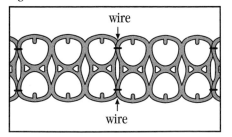

2. Spray paint chain and coat hanger black.

3. For handle, remove cardboard tube from pants hanger; discard wire portion. Use utility knife to cut a 9" length from cardboard tube.

4. Measure around cardboard tube; add 1". Cut a 9¼" long piece from paper bag the determined width. Slightly crumple paper piece; uncrumple paper piece and lay flat. Use foam brush to apply craft glue to 1 side of crumpled paper. Wrap paper piece around cardboard tube. Repeat for desired thickness of handle.

5. Use wire cutters to cut hook section from coat hanger; cut about 3" from each end of remaining hanger piece. Form hanger piece into handle shape. Slide covered cardboard tube onto center of hanger piece. Hot glue ends of handle to inside of shoe box at each end.

6. Fill shoe box with floral foam to about ½" from rim; hot glue to secure.

7. Hot glue sphagnum moss to top of foam and sheet moss to sides of box, covering foam and box completely. Arrange flowers and grass in foam as desired.

8. Overlapping ends at back, wrap chain around sides of box; hot glue to secure.

TASSELED TIEBACKS

These luxurious tiebacks are an easy remedy for plain window decor. Empty medicine bottles are hidden beneath bits and pieces of satin fringe, textured gimp, and twisted cord to add fullness to our drapery accents.

Recycled item: round plastic medicine bottle with lid for each tassel.

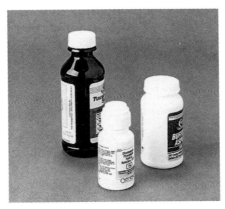

For each tieback, you will also need: bullion fringe (ours is 5" to 7" long); desired cord, desired trims (we used fringe and gimp); a large wooden bead and spray paint (optional); safety pin; cup hook; tape measure; and a hot glue gun and glue sticks.

1. (*Note:* Follow all steps for each tieback. When gluing trims to bottle, match ends of trims at back of bottle. To prevent trim or cord from fraying, apply glue to ½" of trim or cord around area to be cut before cutting.) With top edge of fringe about ½" from bottom of bottle, glue bullion fringe around bottle 2 or 3 times.

2. Working from fringe upward, glue lengths of cord and trim around sides of bottle, covering sides of bottle completely.

3. For hanging loop, cut 1 strand of fringe from bullion fringe. For plain hanging loop, glue ends of fringe strand to top of bottle lid. For hanging loop with bead, spray paint bead, glue ends of fringe strand into bead, and glue bead to bottle lid.

4. To cover lid, coil cord on top of lid, covering ends of hanging loop or edge of bead; glue in place.

5. Glue more trims to tassel as desired.

6. To determine length of tieback, drape tape measure around curtain at desired position of tieback; add 2" to measurement on tape measure. Cut 1 or more lengths of cord, fringe, or other trim the determined measurement. Glue trims together as desired for tieback. Fold each end of tieback 1" to wrong side and glue in place.

7. Screw a cup hook into wall next to curtain at desired height of tieback. Wrap tieback around curtain and use a safety pin to pin ends together. Hang safety pin on hook.

ETCHED GLASS LAMPS

*Y*ou can craft unique lamps with empty glass jars and bottles, etching cream, and lamp kits. Our shades are decorated with pleated wrapping paper or preserved leaves and rope glued to purchased handmade paper.

FLORAL DELIGHT LAMP

Recycled item: 4-pound honey jar.

You will also need: a jar lid lamp kit, glass etching cream, rubber gloves, clear self-adhesive plastic (Con-tact® paper), lampshade to fit lamp, heavy wrapping paper to cover lampshade, 1/4"w satin ribbon, 1/4" hole punch, masking tape, permanent felt-tip pen with fine point, craft knife, and craft glue.

1. Cut a 6" x 8" piece of self-adhesive plastic. Use permanent pen to trace pattern, page 124, onto center of plastic side of self-adhesive plastic.
2. Remove paper backing from plastic. With pattern centered on front of jar, place plastic on jar, smoothing bubbles and wrinkles.

3. Use craft knife to carefully cut along lines of design. Referring to pattern and leaving shaded area of design intact, remove remaining plastic from jar.
4. Cut narrow strips of masking tape to fit across sides of jar; apply to jar (we placed our strips along raised areas on sides of jar).
5. (*Note:* Follow manufacturer's instructions and wear rubber gloves when using etching cream.) Apply etching cream to front and sides of jar. Remove etching cream from jar. Remove plastic and tape from jar.

6. Follow lamp kit manufacturer's instructions to assemble lamp.
7. To cover lampshade, measure from top edge to bottom edge of shade; add 1". Measure around widest part of shade and multiply by 1 1/2. Cut a piece of wrapping paper the determined measurements. Fanfold wrapping paper, making pleats about 1/2"w across width of paper. Overlap 1 pleat at ends of paper piece and glue ends together to from a tube (overlap is back).
8. Punch a hole through each pleat in tube about 1/2" from 1 end (top).

9. Measure around top of shade and multiply by 3. Cut a length of ribbon the determined measurement. Beginning at front, thread ribbon though holes in pleated tube. Place shade on lamp. Place pleated tube over shade and gently pull ends of ribbon, gathering pleats to fit shade. Tie ribbon ends together into a bow; trim ends. Spot glue pleated tube to shade.

GARDEN GREENERY LAMP

Recycled item: wine bottle.

You will also need: a bottle lamp kit, glass etching cream, rubber gloves, clear self-adhesive plastic (Con-tact® paper), self-adhesive lampshade to fit lamp, handmade paper to cover lampshade, preserved leaves, acrylic paint to coordinate with handmade paper, old toothbrush, heavy jute twine, natural raffia, spring-type clothespins, permanent felt-tip pen with fine point, craft knife, tracing paper (optional), and craft glue.

1. Measure around bottle. Measure height of straight part of side of bottle. Cut a piece of self-adhesive plastic the determined measurements.
2. Use permanent pen to trace leaf patterns, page 125, as desired onto plastic side of self-adhesive plastic. For patterns in reverse, trace patterns onto tracing

paper and turn over before tracing onto plastic.
3. Follow Steps 2, 3, 5, and 6 of Floral Delight Lamp instructions to etch bottle and assemble lamp, applying etching cream to entire bottle.
4. (*Note:* Practice spattering technique on scrap paper before painting handmade paper.) To spatter paint paper, dip bristle tips of toothbrush in paint and pull thumb across bristles. Repeat as desired.
5. Follow manufacturer's instructions to cover shade with painted handmade paper.

6. For trim at top of shade, measure around top edge of shade. Cut a length of twine the determined measurement. Beginning at shade seamline, glue twine along top edge of shade. Use clothespins to secure until glue is dry. Repeat for trim at bottom of shade. Glue preserved leaves to shade as desired.
7. Place shade on lamp.
8. Tie a length of raffia into a bow around bottle neck; trim ends.

PAPERED DRESSER

Transform an old dresser into a folk-art heirloom and hardly lift a paintbrush! Checkerboard wallpaper and rustic mural borders are used to cover the top, sides, and drawers of the dresser. For a homey finish, we painted the drawer pulls and added pine bun feet.

Recycled item: wooden dresser.

You will also need: pre-pasted wallpapers (we used a border design on our drawer fronts and coordinating wallpaper on remainder of our dresser); white water-base primer; acrylic paint to coordinate with wallpapers; brown acrylic paint and soft cloth to antique dresser (optional); clear acrylic varnish; assorted round and flat paintbrushes; foam brushes; wallpaper brush or sponge; 4 pine bun feet (optional; available at home centers); fine sandpaper or steel wool; tack cloth; tracing paper; rotary cutter, cutting mat, and ruler (optional); and transparent tape (if needed).

1. Remove drawers from dresser; label drawers for easy reassembly if necessary. Remove pulls from drawers. If replacing feet, remove feet from dresser.
2. To prepare dresser, drawers, pulls, and bun feet for painting, lightly sand or rub steel wool over each piece to smooth any rough areas or to roughen slick surfaces for better paint adhesion; use tack cloth to remove dust.
3. Follow manufacturer's instructions to apply primer to dresser, drawers, pulls, and feet.

4. For painted borders, use a pencil and ruler to lightly mark desired width of borders along edges of each drawer front and top, bottom, and sides of dresser (the borders on our dresser measure about 1/4"w around drawer fronts and about 1 1/4"w around sides and top).
5. For wallpaper pattern for each section of dresser, place tracing paper over dresser section and trace drawn lines on dresser section onto tracing paper (if necessary, use tape to piece tracing paper); cut shape from tracing paper. Label pattern.
6. (*Note:* We recommend using rotary cutter and cutting mat to cut wallpaper pieces.) Placing patterns over desired designs on wallpaper, use patterns to cut pieces from wallpaper.
7. Use desired color(s) of paint and flat paintbrush(es) to paint borders on dresser, painting just over drawn lines to ensure that no gaps will be left between wallpaper pieces and painted border. Paint back of dresser if desired.
8. Follow manufacturer's instructions to apply wallpaper pieces to dresser.
9. Paint drawer pulls and feet as desired.
10. To antique dresser (we antiqued our drawer pulls and feet), mix 1 part brown paint with 1 part water. Working on 1 area of dresser at a time, use foam brush to apply mixture to dresser; use soft cloth to wipe away excess paint. If desired, repeat to make some areas darker.
11. Reattach drawer pulls to dresser. If desired, attach 1 foot to each bottom corner of dresser.
12. Apply 2 to 3 coats of varnish to dresser and drawers.
13. Replace drawers in dresser.

Fun FIX-UPS

Crafters can find inspiration for projects in some of the most unlikely places — such as the household junk drawer, or even the recycling bin! You'll enjoy using an assortment of castaway items to create garden stepping stones, a fishing stool, magazine caddies, and more. This nifty collection includes treasures youngsters will have a blast making, too, from candy wrapper-covered school supplies to game-piece picture frames. Fashioning crafty fix-ups is fun when you put your heart (and discards) into it!

CANDY WRAPPER COVER-UPS

*C*reate way-cool desk necessities for home or school using wrappers from your kids' favorite candies. Their classmates are sure to go nuts over the novelty three-ring binder, pencils, and supply keepers!

CANDY WRAPPER DECOUPAGE

Recycled items: candy wrappers, 3-ring binder and paper for background (we used a sack from a fast-food restaurant) for notebook, a cardboard snack canister with lid and a plastic screw-on lid from bottle for canister, and a cigar box for supply box.

You will also need: decoupage glue (either use purchased glue or mix 1 part craft glue with 1 part water to make glue), foam brush, soft cloths, and clear acrylic spray.

For canister, you will also need: desired colors of spray paint for lid, a 1¹/₂" dia. wooden bead for head, black permanent felt-tip pen with fine point, and a hot glue gun and glue sticks.

For each pencil, you will also need: an unsharpened pencil.

NOTEBOOK
1. For background, open notebook flat and cut a piece of paper for background same size as notebook. Use foam brush to apply glue to front of notebook. Apply paper to front of notebook and smooth in place, working from center outward. With

notebook closed and working around binding to back of notebook, continue applying glue and paper to notebook until notebook is covered.

2. Follow *Decoupage* instructions, page 127, to decoupage notebook with candy wrappers.

CANISTER

1. Follow *Decoupage* instructions, page 127, to decoupage canister.

2. For lid, spray paint lid of canister, bead, and bottle lid for hat desired colors.

3. Use black pen to draw face on bead. Hot glue bottle lid to top of bead for hat. Hot glue bead to center of canister lid.

SUPPLY BOX

Follow *Decoupage* instructions, page 127, to decoupage box.

PENCIL

Follow *Decoupage* instructions, page 127, to decoupage wooden part of pencil.

CRAFTY TOTES

*F*abric-covered detergent boxes enhanced with pockets and handles make handy helpers for seamstresses and crafters on the go! The sewing tote features a pincushion and a needle case, and the artist's carrier, shown on page 96, has handy paintbrush holders. These clever totes are just right for keeping all kinds of crafting necessities!

CRAFT TOTES

Recycled items: buttons and a detergent box with fold-down lid for each tote.
For each tote, you will also need: fabrics for lining and pockets, thread, 3/4"w paper-twist braid for handle, assorted narrow-width ribbons, embroidery floss, utility knife, tracing paper, spray adhesive, and a hot glue gun and glue sticks.
For sewing tote, you will also need: fabrics to cover box, a 2 1/2" dia. plastic foam half-ball and 1" x 6" torn fabric strips for pincushion, jute twine, fabric marking pen, embroidery needle, and a 1/2" dia. adhesive-backed hook and loop fastener.
For painting tote, you will also need: canvas to cover box, desired colors of acrylic paint, and paintbrushes.

SEWING TOTE
1. If box has a handle, remove it.
2. (*Note:* If lid hinges below top of box like the one in Fig. 1, follow Step 2. If lid hinges at top of box like the one in Fig. 2, skip to Step 3.) Referring to areas shown in red in Fig. 3, page 95, use utility knife

to cut away part of each side of box lid. Hot glue back of lid to back of box so lid hinges at top of box.

Fig. 1

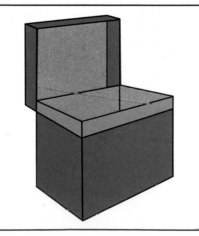

Fig. 2

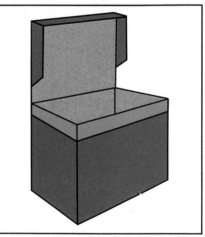

Fig. 3

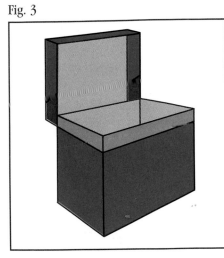

Fig. 4

3. (*Note:* Refer to Fig. 4 to measure box.) Measure box from bottom edge of front of lid around box to top edge of front of lid (shown by blue arrow); add 5". Measure from bottom of 1 side of lid over top of lid to bottom of remaining side (shown by red arrow); add 3". Cut a piece of fabric the determined measurements.

4. (*Note:* Use hot glue for all gluing unless otherwise indicated.) Apply spray adhesive to wrong side of fabric. With back bottom edge of box centered across wrong side of fabric, place box on fabric. Wrap fabric around box and press in place. Referring to Fig. 5, press fabric together at front corners of lid, make clips in fabric where lid meets box, and

fold fabric at sides of box gift-wrap style and press in place. Fold excess fabric at front and sides of box to inside of box.

Fig. 5

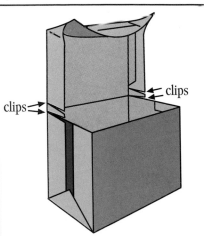

clips
clips

5. Referring to Fig. 6, fold excess fabric at front corners of lid to sides and then to inside of lid. Glue fabric in place at overlaps.

Fig. 6

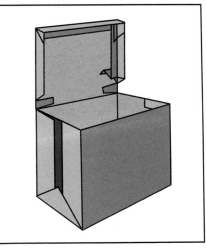

6. To cover each side of box, measure width of side of box; add 1". Measure height of side of box; add 3". Cut a piece of fabric the determined measurements. Press 1 short and long edges of fabric piece 1/2" to wrong side. Apply spray adhesive to wrong side of fabric piece.

With short pressed edge at bottom of box, smooth fabric piece in place on side of box, folding excess fabric to inside of box.

7. To line inside of lid, measure inside top of lid from front to back; add 3". Measure inside top of lid from side to side and add 1". Cut a piece of fabric the determined measurements. Press 1 long and both short edges of fabric piece 1/2" to wrong side. Apply spray adhesive to wrong side of fabric piece. Match pressed edges of fabric piece to front and side edges of inside top of box lid and press fabric piece in place (excess fabric will extend into box).

8. To line bottom of box, measure length and width of bottom of box; add 1" to each measurement. Cut a piece of fabric the determined measurements. Press edges 1/2" to wrong side. Apply spray adhesive to wrong side of fabric piece and press into bottom of box.

9. To line sides of box, measure around inside of tote; add 1". Measure height of inside of tote; add 1". Cut a piece of fabric the determined measurements. Press 1 short and long edges 1/2" to wrong side. Apply spray adhesive to wrong side of fabric piece. Beginning with raw edge of fabric piece about 1/2" beyond 1 corner of box, press fabric onto sides inside box.

10. Glue overlapped edges of fabric in place as necessary.

11. (*Note:* Follow Steps 11 - 13 for each side pocket. Use a 1/4" seam allowance for sewing steps unless otherwise indicated.) Cut two 5" x 6" fabric pieces. Place fabric pieces right sides together. Leaving an opening for turning, sew pieces together. Clip seam allowance at corners and turn shape right side out; press. Hand sew opening closed. Refer to Fig. 7, page 97, to press a pleat along center of shape; pin bottom of pleat to secure. Topstitch 1/8" from all edges of shape, securing bottom of pleat. Remove pin.

Fig. 7

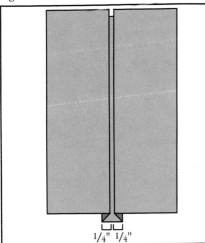

1/4" 1/4"

12. For flap on pocket, use pocket flap pattern, page 125, and follow *Sewing Shapes*, page 127, to make flap from fabrics. Press flap and hand stitch opening closed. Topstitch 1/8" from edges of flap. Press top 2 1/2" of flap to back. Sew a button to point of flap.

13. Glue back of flap to side of tote. Glue side and bottom edges of pocket to tote over back of flap about 3/4" from fold in flap.

14. For scissors pocket, cut two 4" x 8" pieces each from fabrics for pocket and lining. Matching right sides, place 1 lining fabric piece on each pocket fabric piece. Sew each pair of fabric pieces together along 1 short edge (top). Matching raw edges, turn each pair of fabric pieces right side out and press. Place sewn fabric pieces together with lining sides out; pin to secure. Trace scissors pocket pattern, page 125, onto tracing paper; cut out. Matching top edge of pattern to top (seamed edge) of fabric pieces, use fabric marking pen to draw around pattern on fabric. Sew fabric pieces together along drawn lines. Leaving a 1/4" seam allowance, cut out pocket. Clip curves, turn right side out, and press. Glue pocket to front of tote.

15. For pattern pocket on back of tote, measure width of back of tote; measure height of back of tote and subtract 1". Cut 2 pieces of fabric the determined measurements. Place fabric pieces right sides together. Leaving an opening for turning, sew fabric pieces together. Turn right side out and press; hand stitch opening closed. Topstitch 1/8" from edges of pocket. Center pocket on back of tote close to bottom edge; glue side and bottom edges of pocket to tote.

16. For needle case, cut the following strips from fabrics: two 4 x 6 1/4" and one 4" x 12". Place short strips right sides together. Sew strips together along 1 short edge. Unfold strip and press seam allowance open. Trace needle case pattern, page 125, onto tracing paper; extend square end of pattern 3". Cut out pattern. Use pattern and follow *Sewing Shapes*, page 127, to make needle case from solid and pieced fabric strips. Press needle case and hand stitch opening closed. Press pointed end of needle case (flap) 2 3/4" toward solid side (inside); press remaining end 3 7/8" toward inside. Sew a button to point of flap. Adhere 1 part of hook and loop fastener to inside of flap at point. Making sure parts of fastener will meet, adhere remaining part of fastener to front of case. Glue back of case to top of tote.

17. For pincushion, cover foam half-ball with torn fabric strips, gluing ends of strips to flat side and covering foam completely. Glue flat side to top of tote.

18. For tote handle, use a tape measure to determine desired length of handle; add 2". Cut a length of braid the determined measurement. Apply glue to ends of braid to prevent fraying.

19. (*Note:* Follow Step 19 for each side of handle.) Use utility knife to cut a small hole in side of tote at desired height of handle end. Thread needle with 6 strands of floss. Begin on inside of tote and bring needle through 1 button inside tote, side of tote, 1 end of braid, and another button. Thread needle back through button, braid, tote, and first button. Repeat stitching several times. Pull ends of floss tightly and knot on inside of tote.

20. For bow, cut several 16" lengths of ribbon and jute. Holding jute and ribbon together, follow Steps 1 - 3 of *Making a Multi-Loop Bow*, page 127, to make bow. Knot another ribbon length around center of bow to secure loops. Glue bow to front of tote. Thread ends of ribbons and jute though buttons; knot and trim ends.

PAINTING TOTE

1. Use paints and paintbrushes to paint 1 side (right side) of canvas as desired.

2. Using canvas to cover outside of tote, follow Steps 1 - 13 of Sewing Tote instructions.

3. (*Note:* Follow Step 3 for each paintbrush pocket.) Cut two 5" x 6" fabric pieces. Fold 1 short edge (top) of each fabric piece 1/2" to wrong side; press. Matching right sides and pressed edges, sew raw edges of fabric pieces together. Clip corners, turn right side out, and press. To divide pocket into sections, stitch lines at desired intervals from top to bottom of pocket. Glue pocket to tote.

4. For handle, follow Step 18 of Sewing Tote instructions. Paint approx. 1 1/2"w sections on braid desired colors.

5. To attach handle to tote, follow Step 19 of Sewing Tote instructions.

6. For bow, cut several 16" lengths of ribbon. Holding ribbon lengths together, follow Steps 1 - 3 of *Making a Multi-Loop Bow*, page 127, to make bow. Knot another ribbon length around center of bow to secure loops. Glue bow to front of tote. Trim ribbon ends.

Homey Address Plaque

Personalized by you, our homey sign will make a delightful housewarming gift for new homeowners! Plain ceramic tiles are painted and displayed in a wooden frame to create this striking address plaque.

Address Plaque

Recycled items: 4¹/₄" square ceramic tiles.

You will also need: a frame with backing and hanging hardware to hold tiles (we purchased our frame, which is designed to hold tiles, at a home center), desired colors of Liquitex® Glossies acrylic enamel paint, small paintbrushes, lettering stencils (optional), and household cement.

1. Arrange tiles in a row. Use a pencil (and lettering stencils if desired) to sketch desired designs and address on tiles (we sketched squares, simple flower and leaf shapes, and curly numbers and letters on our tiles.) Paint designs on tiles.

2. Glue tiles into frame.

3. Follow manufacturer's instructions to attach hanging hardware to frame.

PIZZA-BOX STEPPING STONES

*D*elivered right to your door along with supper are the perfect forms for making expensive-looking stepping stones! Brick mortar is inlaid with small rocks or a handwritten message and allowed to harden in sturdy take-out pizza boxes. These outdoor accents will add a winsome touch to your garden path.

GARDEN TILES

Recycled items: 4 wire coat hangers for each tile and approx. 13" take-out pizza boxes (one box may be used to make 2 to 3 tiles).

You will also need: brick mortar mix (available at home centers), a large heavy-duty garbage bag, coarse sandpaper, small rocks (optional), utility knife, and 2"w packing tape.

1. Use utility knife to cut lid from box.
2. To strengthen sides of box, apply several layers of tape to top edges and sides of box.

3. Cut a square from garbage bag about 3" larger on all sides than box. Line box with plastic square.
4. To reinforce mortar, refer to Fig. 1 to place hangers in bottom of box.

Fig. 1

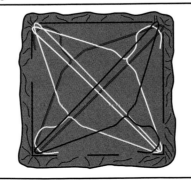

5. Follow manufacturer's instructions to mix mortar; pour mortar into box, filling box to about ¹/₂" from top. Before mortar sets up, use either finger or a stick to write message in mortar or press small rocks into mortar, smoothing mortar around rocks. Allow mortar to set completely.
6. Using edges of plastic to lift tile, remove tile from box. Remove plastic from bottom of tile. If necessary, use sandpaper to smooth edges of tile.

Brown paper bags are "recycled" to make the cheery blooms on our sunny wreath. Faux berries, small clay flowerpots, and a watering can also decorate this summertime accent.

Recycled items: brown paper lunch and grocery bags and either newspaper or plastic grocery bags.

You will also need: a 25" dia. grapevine wreath; desired artificial vines, berry sprigs, and greenery (we used latex raspberry vines, strawberry and blueberry sprigs, and artificial grass); assorted small clay pots; a 5"h aluminum watering can; black spray paint; yellow, yellow orange, orange, tan, brown, and dark brown acrylic paint; small sponge pieces; chenille stems; paper towels; tracing paper; and a hot glue gun and glue sticks.

1. Lightly spray paint watering can black to antique.

2. (*Note:* Follow Steps 2 - 6 for each sunflower.) For flower center, firmly stuff bottom 2" of a lunch bag with crumpled newspaper or plastic grocery bags. Twist bag at top of newspaper and form stuffed part of bag into an approx. 4" dia. flattened ball; secure with a chenille stem. Trim excess bag close to chenille stem.

3. To sponge paint flower center, dip dampened sponge piece into brown paint; remove excess on a paper towel. Using a light stamping motion so bag shows through, use sponge piece to paint flower center. Repeat with tan, then dark brown paint.

4. For petals, cut along 1 side fold and cut bottom from grocery bag; unfold bag and lay flat. Follow Step 3 to sponge paint bag using yellow, yellow orange, and orange paint.

5. Trace petal patterns, page 126, onto tracing paper; cut out. Use patterns to cut 7 small and 8 large petals from painted bag.

6. To assemble flower, glue straight ends of smaller petals around flower center close to chenille stem. Repeat to glue larger petals behind smaller petals.

7. Glue vines, berry sprigs, greenery, and clay pots to wreath as desired. Glue sunflowers to 1 side of wreath. Glue watering can to bottom of wreath.

NOVELTY CANISTER BANKS

Saving for a rainy day or an upcoming vacation? Or do you just like having mad money on hand? Either way, you'll love our clever little banks! Empty food canisters are decorated with fabrics, postcards, or play money for these whimsical currency keepers. They're a fun way to stash your cash!

COIN BANKS

Recycled items: metal cocoa container for rainy day bank, cardboard salt container and postcards for vacation fund bank, or plastic cocoa container for money bank.

You will also need: a hot glue gun and glue sticks.

For rainy day bank, you will also need: desired spray paint for top of container and heart, fabric to cover bank, paper-backed fusible web, a 2¹/8"w wooden heart cutout, a black felt-tip pen with medium point, a hand drill with a ³/8" metal bit, tin snips or wire cutters, a metal file, and poster board.

For vacation fund bank, you will also need: 1¹/2"w grosgrain ribbon, a craft pick, craft knife, dimensional paint, and craft glue.

For money bank, you will also need: desired spray paint for lid, craft knife, large play dollar bills, plastic coins, and craft glue.

RAINY DAY BANK

1. For coin slot, remove lid from container. Use drill to drill 2 holes about 3/8" apart at center of lid. Draw 2 straight lines connecting sides of holes. Use tin snips to cut out slot along drawn lines. Use file to smooth edges of cut metal.
2. Spray paint heart cutout, lid, and top of container. Replace lid on container.
3. Follow manufacturer's instructions to fuse web to wrong side of fabric.
4. Measure height of container. Measure around container and add 1/2". Cut a piece of poster board the determined measurements. Cut a piece of fabric 1/2" larger on all sides than poster board. Remove paper backing.
5. Center poster board on wrong side of fabric. Press short edges, then long edges of fabric to back of poster board and fuse in place. Turn poster board over and fuse fabric to front of poster board.
6. Overlapping short edges at back of container, glue fabric-covered poster board around container.
7. Use black pen to write "for a rainy day" on heart; glue heart to bank.

VACATION FUND BANK

1. For top of container, remove metal spout from container. Draw around top of container on back of 1 postcard. Cut circle from postcard. Use craft glue to glue circle to top of container.
2. For coin slot, use craft knife to cut an approx. 3/8" x 1 1/8" slot in top of container.
3. Overlapping ends at back, hot glue lengths of ribbon along top and bottom edges of container.
4. Hot glue additional postcards to sides of container to cover container, trimming edges of postcards as desired.
5. For flag, cut a 6" length of ribbon. Cut notches in each ribbon end. Hot glue large end of craft pick at center on wrong side of ribbon. Fold ribbon in half and hot glue ends of ribbon together at an angle. Use dimensional paint to write "vacation fund" on flag. Use craft knife to make a small hole in top of container. Insert end of flag into hole and hot glue to secure.

MONEY BANK

1. For coin slot, use craft knife to cut an approx. 3/8" x 1 1/8" slot in center of lid.
2. Spray paint lid.
3. Use craft glue to glue bills around sides of container. Hot glue coins to top of container along edges of coin slot and to front of container.

*I*t's "sew" easy to tailor-make a bulletin board to coordinate with your decor! Cardboard forms from fabric bolts are simply taped together, covered with batting and fabric, and embellished with a crisscrossing grid of elastic and buttons.

Recycled items: 2 same-size empty fabric bolts for 44/45"w fabric (found at fabric stores), corrugated cardboard, and 5 large buttons.

You will also need: fabric, high-loft polyester bonded batting, 4 yds of ³⁄₈"w elastic, upholstery needle, quilting thread to match fabric, awl, 24" of picture hanging wire, duct tape, and a hot glue gun and glue sticks.

1. For board, place fabric bolts side by side on a flat surface, matching 2 long edges. Securely tape bolts together.

2. Draw around board on cardboard twice. Cut out 1 cardboard shape just inside drawn lines. Cut out second shape 1" inside drawn lines; set smaller cardboard shape aside for backing.

3. Cut larger cardboard shape in half lengthwise. Center 1 piece over taped area on each side of board to stabilize; glue to secure.

4. Measure width and height of board; add 6" to each measurement. Cut a piece of fabric the determined measurements. Cut a piece of batting 1" smaller on all sides than fabric.

5. Center batting on wrong side of fabric. Center board on batting. Pulling fabric taut, fold long, then short edges of fabric to back of board and glue in place, folding fabric at corners as necessary.

6. For holding straps, cut elastic into two 32" lengths and four 20" lengths. Arrange elastic lengths on board to form a grid; pin in place. Glue ends of elastic to back of board to secure.

7. For each button, place button on bulletin board over 1 intersection of elastic and use a pencil to mark holes in button on elastic. Use awl to make a hole through board at each mark. Stitching through holes, use upholstery needle and quilting thread to sew buttons to board. Knot thread and trim ends at back.

8. For backing, cut a piece of fabric 2" larger on all sides than remaining cardboard piece. Center cardboard on wrong side of fabric. Fold and glue edges of fabric to back of cardboard.

9. For hanger, use awl to make 2 holes at center of backing about 8" apart and about 5" from 1 short edge (top). Thread wire through holes and securely twist ends together on wrong side of backing. Center and glue backing to back of bulletin board.

SEWING CARD CUTOUTS

*S*ure to keep youngsters entertained, our cute sewing cards are super easy to make! Old calendar illustrations are simply glued to poster board and cut out. Kids can then sew lengths of colorful ribbon through holes punched in the cards.

CHILDREN'S SEWING CARDS

Recycled item: wall picture calendar.
You will also need: poster board, 1/4"w satin ribbon, 1/4" hole punch, spring-type clothespins, spray adhesive, and fabric glue.

1. (*Note:* Follow all steps for each card.) Use spray adhesive to glue 1 calendar picture page to poster board. Cut desired shape from poster board.
2. Punch pairs of holes about 1 1/2" apart along edges of shape.
3. Measure around edges of cutout; add 20". Cut a length of ribbon the determined measurement.
4. To stiffen each end of ribbon, apply fabric glue to about 1" of ribbon end and fold end in half lengthwise; use a clothespin to secure until glue is dry.
5. "Sew" ribbon through holes in card. Tie ends into a bow.

NIFTY NECKLACES

Little girls will have a ball creating these fun fashion accessories — and it's a great activity for a birthday party or sleepover! Strung with beads and glittery packing foam pieces, lengths of satin raffia become nifty necklace favors.

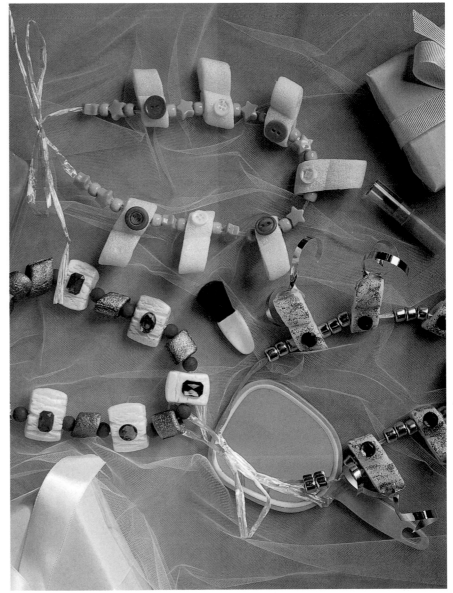

KIDS' FUN NECKLACES

Note: These necklaces were designed to be fun and easy for children to make. For young children, you may want to paint foam pieces so necklaces will be ready to assemble.

Recycled items: packing foam pieces and buttons (optional).

You will also need: Darice® Straw Satin Radiant Raffia Straw, assorted beads, and children's plastic craft needles.
You may also need: metallic gold curling ribbon, metallic gold acrylic spray paint, iridescent or glitter acrylic paint, lengths of heavy gauge floral wire, small paintbrush, small acrylic jewels, and jewel glue.

1. For painted foam pieces, thread foam pieces onto a length of wire to hold in place while painting. Either spray paint foam pieces or brush a light coat of iridescent or glitter paint on foam pieces.
2. For decorated foam pieces, glue jewels or buttons to foam pieces. If desired, thread short lengths of curling ribbon through holes in foam pieces, knot

ribbons close to foam pieces, and curl ribbon ends.
3. (*Note:* Follow Step 3 for each necklace.) Thread needle with a 1-yd length of raffia and knot 1 end. String foam pieces and beads onto raffia. Unthread needle and knot remaining end. Tie ends into a bow.

PICTURESQUE TREASURE BOXES

*N*ow you can create *photo storage boxes like the ones found in department stores — for just pennies! Decorated with an array of old maps, wrapping paper scraps, and color photocopies of snapshots, shoe boxes are ideal holders for treasured photographs.*

PHOTOGRAPH STORAGE BOXES

Recycled items: sturdy shoe boxes, wrapping paper, and maps.

You will also need: decoupage glue (either use purchased glue or mix 1 part craft glue with 1 part water to make glue), foam brush, soft cloths, and clear acrylic spray.

For map-covered box, you will also need: either word, phrase, or picture cutouts from magazines for labels; colored paper for label backgrounds; and brown acrylic paint and a foam brush to antique box (optional).

For paper-covered box, you will also need: wrapping paper; decorative brass corners; a 1¼" x 2⅞" white paper piece,

a 1½" x 3⅛" brown paper piece, a black felt-tip pen with fine point, and a gold paint pen for label (optional); and a hot glue gun and glue sticks.

For photo-covered box, you will also need: desired color spray paint (we used black), desired colors of acrylic paint for dots, pencil with unused eraser, cutouts from color photocopies of photograph(s), and photocopy of label, page 126 (optional).

MAP-COVERED BOX

1. (*Note:* To cover box with a whole map, follow Steps 1 - 6. To cover box with sections cut from maps follow Steps 1

and 2 of *Decoupage* instructions, page 127.) To cover box lid, measure length and width of lid, including sides and ends (Fig. 1); add 3" to each measurement. Cut a piece from map the determined measurements.

Fig. 1

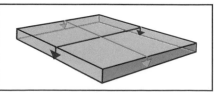

2. Center lid top side down on wrong side of map piece. Use a pencil to draw around lid; remove lid. Draw lines 1"

outside original drawn shape as shown in Fig. 2. Cut away corners of map piece and make a diagonal clip at each corner from outer drawn lines to about $^1/_{16}$" from original drawn shape (Fig. 3).

Fig. 2

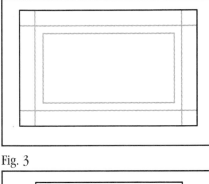

Fig. 3

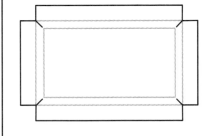

3. (*Note:* Use decoupage glue for all gluing unless otherwise indicated.) Use foam brush to apply glue to top of box lid. Center lid on map piece. Turn lid over and press map piece in place.

4. To cover each side of lid, apply glue to side of lid; press map piece onto side of lid. Referring to Fig. 4, apply glue to ends of lid; press ends of map piece onto ends of lid. Fold excess paper to inside and glue in place.

Fig. 4

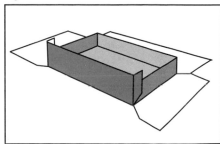

5. To cover each end of lid, fold short edges of map piece at 1 end of lid 1" to wrong side (Fig. 5). Apply glue to end of lid. Press map piece onto end of lid. Fold excess paper to inside and glue in place.

Fig. 5

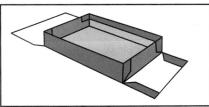

6. Repeat Steps 1 - 5 to cover box.
7. To antique box, spray box with clear acrylic spray. Mix 1 part brown paint with 1 part water. Working on 1 area at a time, use a clean foam brush to apply mixture to box; use a soft cloth to wipe away excess paint.
8. For labels, either glue magazine cutouts to box or glue cutouts to paper, cut out paper about $^1/_8$" from edges of cutouts, and glue to box.
9. Spray box with several coats of clear acrylic spray.

PAPER-COVERED BOX
1. To cover box with wrapping paper, follow Steps 1 - 6 of Map-covered Box instructions.
2. For label, use black pen to write "PHOTOGRAPHS" on white paper. Glue white paper to brown paper. Use gold pen to draw lines from corners of white paper to corners brown paper. Glue label to box.
3. Spray box with several coats of clear acrylic spray.
4. Hot glue brass corners to lid.

PHOTO-COVERED BOX
1. Spray paint box and lid.
2. Follow Steps 1 and 2 of *Decoupage* instructions, page 127, to decoupage box and lid with photocopy cutouts.
3. Use unused pencil eraser dipped in paint to paint dots on box as desired.
4. For label, cut out photocopy of label and glue to box.
5. Spray box with several coats of clear acrylic spray.

PHOTO FRAME PIZZAZZ

These whimsical projects are perfect for displaying snapshots of your children! You can use old markers, orphaned game pieces, and empty compact disk and cassette tape cases to fashion photo frames with pizzazz.

PHOTO FRAMES

Recycled items: either 4 rectangular highlighter markers; checker, domino, chess, and other game pieces; or an empty cassette tape or compact disc case.

You will also need: either a photograph or color photocopy of one and a hot glue gun and glue sticks.

For marker frame, you will also need: two 1¼" dia. wooden beads for feet, assorted beads for decoration, acrylic paint, paintbrushes, and lightweight cardboard.

110

For game pieces frame, you will also need: tracing paper, lightweight cardboard, a craft knife and cutting mat or folded newspaper, and a craft glue stick.

For music frames, you will also need: ribbon and items to decorate frame (we used 5/8"w black and white dotted grosgrain ribbon and miniature records, gummed stars, a music note decoration, and a sequin star); and two 1¼" dia. wooden beads, acrylic paint, paintbrush, and dimensional paint (for feet on compact disc frame).

MARKER FRAME

1. (*Note:* This frame is designed to fit an approx. 4" square photograph.) For frame back, arrange markers in a square on cardboard. Draw around outer edges of markers; cut out cardboard shape about ⅛" inside drawn lines.

2. Glue marker tops in place to secure. Center and glue 1 marker along each side edge of cardboard square. Apply a thick line of glue near bottom edge of cardboard (to support bottom edge of photo). Glue remaining markers to markers on cardboard, centering markers over top and bottom edges of frame.

3. Paint beads as desired.

4. For feet, glue one 1¼" dia. bead to each bottom corner of frame. Glue remaining beads to frame as desired to decorate.

5. Insert photograph in frame, trimming to fit as necessary.

GAME PIECES FRAME

1. For frame, cut a piece of tracing paper same size as photograph. Use craft glue stick to glue tracing paper piece to cardboard. Arrange flat game pieces as desired over edges of tracing paper piece to form basic frame shape; glue in place.

Use craft knife and cutting mat to cut out frame along inner and outer edges of game pieces.

2. For frame back, draw around outer edges of frame on cardboard; cut out shape just inside drawn lines.

3. For feet, stack and glue flat game pieces together; glue to bottom of frame. Glue additional game pieces to frame as desired.

4. Gluing along side and bottom edges only, glue frame back to frame. Insert photograph in frame.

MUSIC FRAMES

1. Place cassette tape or compact disc case over area of photograph to be framed. Use a pencil to draw around case. Cut out photograph just inside drawn lines.

2. Place photograph in case and use small dots of glue at corners to secure.

3. Glue ribbon along sides or front edges of case. Glue decorative items to case.

4. For feet on compact disc frame, paint beads with acrylic paint. Use dimensional paint to paint dots on beads. Glue 1 bead to each bottom corner of case.

BUTTONED-UP PILLOWS

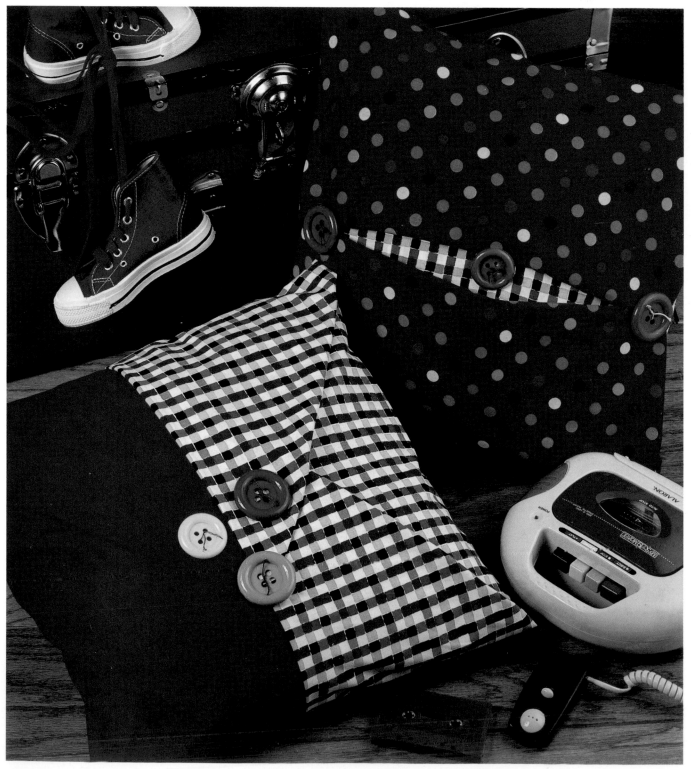

Wrapped in vibrant fabrics, old pillows are transformed into playful accents for the youngsters' rooms. Both the envelope and the fabric band pillow can be finished in a flash. Embellished with oversize buttons, the cute cover-ups are a colorful must!

COVERED PILLOWS

Recycled item: square pillow.
You will also need: fabrics, 3/4"w paper-backed fusible web tape, and oversize buttons and embroidery floss to coordinate with fabrics.

ENVELOPE PILLOW

1. Measure pillow from side seam to side seam; add 2³/₄". Measure pillow from top seam to bottom seam; multiply by 2¹/₂. Cut a piece from 2 different fabrics the determined measurements.
2. To piece fabric pieces together, follow manufacturer's instructions to fuse a length of web tape along 1 long edge on right side of each fabric piece. Remove paper backing. Matching right sides and taped edges, fuse fabric pieces together. Press seam allowance to 1 side.
3. Press long edges, then short edges of fabric piece ¹/₂" to wrong side.
4. Center pillow on wrong side of fabric piece. Fold long edges of fabric to center of pillow, overlapping edges; use embroidery floss to tack edges together.
5. For flaps, refer to Fig. 1 to fold ends of fabric piece to form points.

Fig. 1

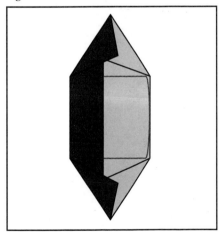

6. Fold bottom flap to center of pillow; tack in place. Fold top flap to center of pillow. Sew buttons to pillow over flaps, knotting and trimming floss at front of each button.

FABRIC BAND PILLOW

1. Measure pillow from side seam to side seam; multiply by 2 and add 6". Cut a square of fabric the determined measurement.
2. Press 2 opposite edges (side edges) of fabric square 1" to wrong side.
3. Center pillow on wrong side of fabric square. Fold side edges of fabric to center of pillow, overlapping edges; use embroidery floss to tack edges together.
4. For fabric band, measure around pillow and add 2¹/₂". Cut a 5¹/₂"w fabric strip the determined measurement. Follow manufacturer's instructions to fuse web tape along edges on wrong side of fabric strip. Press long, then short edges to wrong side along inner edges of web tape. Unfold edges and remove paper backing. Refold edges and fuse in place. With ends overlapping at center front of pillow, wrap band around pillow. To secure ends of band together, use embroidery floss to sew a button to band at overlap, knotting and trimming floss at front of button.
5. For flaps, refer to Fig. 2 and fold raw edges of fabric 3" to wrong side; fold corners of each raw edge under toward center of flap.

Fig. 2

6. Fold flaps to center of pillow. Pull corners of flaps together and overlap slightly; sew a button over each overlap to secure. Slightly fold center of each flap to wrong side at pillow center to expose fabric band.

MAGAZINE CADDY COLLAGES

*D*ecoupaged with a collage of cutouts from wrapping paper, catalogs, and magazines, detergent boxes make nifty holders for your collections of periodicals. These crafty caddies are inexpensive to create — and so much more interesting than plain purchased ones!

MAGAZINE HOLDERS

Recycled items: an approx. 5"w x 9"l detergent box and any combination of the following to decoupage box: wrapping paper, catalogs, or magazines.

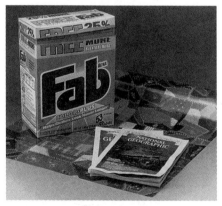

You will also need: decoupage glue (either use purchased glue or mix 1 part craft glue with 1 part water to make glue), foam brush, soft cloths, clear acrylic spray, white paper and a felt-tip pen with fine point for label (optional), and a utility knife.

1. Use a pencil and ruler to draw a line across 1 side of box about 7¹/₂" from bottom. Draw a line across opposite side of box about 4¹/₂" from bottom. Draw lines across front and back of box,

connecting lines on side of box. Referring to Fig. 1, use utility knife to cut off top of box along drawn lines; discard top.

Fig. 1

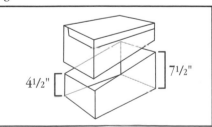

2. Follow Steps 1 and 2 of *Decoupage* instructions, page 127, to decoupage box.
3. For label, either cut name from cover of magazine or cut desired shape from paper and use felt-tip pen to write name or type of magazines on paper. Glue label to tall side of box.
4. Spray box with several coats of clear acrylic spray.

PHOTOGENIC SUNGLASSES

*E*ver wondered what to do with those old, scratched-up sunglasses? Why not use them to create mini photo frames! We simply trimmed photographs to fit in the lens spaces and then glued them in place. Personalized messages add fun to these stand-out accents.

PHOTO FRAME SUNGLASSES

Recycled item: sunglasses (with or without lenses).

You will also need: either photographs or color photocopies of photographs small enough to fit in frames of sunglasses, tracing paper, and craft glue stick.

For frames with lenses, you will also need: dimensional paint.

For frames without lenses, you will also need: poster board, beads and thread (optional), and a hot glue gun and glue sticks.

Note: Top of glasses is bottom of frame.

FRAMES WITH LENSES
1. For photograph pattern, place a small piece of tracing paper over 1 lens of sunglasses and trace shape of lens; cut out.
2. Use pattern to cut desired area from photograph.
3. Apply a thin coat of glue to back of photograph and front of lens; press photograph onto lens. Use fingertips to smooth any wrinkles or bubbles, working from center of photograph outward.
4. Use dimensional paint to paint a decorative line along edges of photograph to secure photograph to lens. Paint name or occasion on remaining lens.

FRAMES WITHOUT LENSES
1. (*Note:* Follow Steps 1 - 4 for each photograph.) For photograph pattern, draw around outer edges of 1 side of sunglasses frames on tracing paper; cut out.
2. Use pattern to cut desired area from photograph.
3. Use glue stick to glue photograph to poster board. Trim poster board even with edges of photograph.
4. Hot glue photograph to back of sunglasses frame.
5. If desired, string beads onto thread to fit along top of 1 side of sunglasses frames; knot thread close to beads. Hot glue ends of thread to sides of frames to secure. Repeat for remaining side of sunglasses.

TOY TOTES

Decoupaged detergent boxes embellished with catalog cutouts make terrific tagalong toy totes! These colorful carryalls are sturdy enough to carry a youngster's favorite playthings, yet small enough to take anywhere.

Recycled items: magazines, catalogs, and a detergent box with fold-down lid.

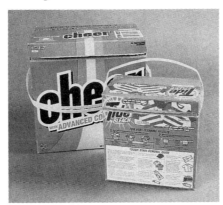

You will also need: acrylic spray paint, ribbon about the same width as side of lid on box for trim, ribbon and beads for handle (optional), foam brush, soft cloths, craft knife, clear acrylic spray, white and black paper and a black felt-tip pen with medium point for label (optional), decoupage glue (either use purchased glue or mix 1 part craft glue with 1 part water to make glue), and a hot glue gun and glue sticks.

1. If replacing handle, remove handle from box.
2. Spray paint inside and outside of box.
3. (*Note:* Use decoupage glue for all gluing unless otherwise indicated.) Follow *Decoupage* instructions, page 127, to decoupage tote with motifs cut from magazines and catalogs.
4. If label is desired, cut desired shape from white paper. Glue desired motif to center of paper. Use black pen to write name and words on paper. Glue white paper piece to black paper. Cutting about 1/8" from white paper, cut out label. Glue label to front of tote.
5. Spray tote with several coats of clear acrylic spray.
6. For trim on lid, measure around sides and front of lid; add 1". Cut a length of ribbon the determined measurement. Hot glue ends 1/2" to wrong side; glue ribbon to sides and front of lid.
7. To add handle to box, use craft knife to cut approx. 1/2" slits in each side of tote at desired height of handle. Use a tape measure to determine desired length of handle; add 4". Cut a length of ribbon the determined measurement. Thread beads onto center of ribbon; knot ribbon close to beads. Insert 1 end of ribbon into each slit; knot and trim ribbon ends on inside of tote. For bow on each side of tote, tie a ribbon length into a bow around handle close to side of tote; trim ribbon ends.

MOSAIC FLOWERPOTS

*T*ransform everyday flowerpots into fanciful patio accents using broken china pieces. These projects let you use chipped or orphaned pieces of china that you just can't bear to throw away! China pieces are glued to the rims or sides of the pots to create the mosaic look.

BROKEN-CHINA FLOWERPOTS

Recycled items: clay flowerpot or saucer and china or broken china pieces.

You will also need: thick craft glue, tile grout, old pillowcase or towel, hammer, and a tile sander.

1. (*Note:* Handle broken china with care.) Place china in pillowcase or wrap in towel; use hammer to break china into small pieces. Use tile sander to sand sharp edges of china pieces.
2. Glue china pieces to flowerpot as desired.
3. After glue is dry, follow manufacturer's instructions to apply grout between and around china pieces on flowerpot.

FISHERMAN'S BUCKET SEAT

*D*ecorated with paper fish cutouts, this sporty stool will be quite a catch for your favorite fisherman! A padded blue jean seat is added to the lid of a large, sturdy plastic bucket to create this handy angler's seat.

FISHING STOOL

Recycled items: denim jeans, a 10-gallon plastic bucket with lid, and corrugated cardboard.

You will also need: decoupage paper with fish motifs, decoupage glue (either use purchased glue or mix 1 part craft glue with 1 part water to make glue), foam brush, soft cloths, clear acrylic spray, high-loft polyester bonded batting, and a hot glue gun and glue sticks.

1. Follow *Decoupage* instructions, page 127, to decoupage bucket with fish motifs.

2. For seat, draw around top of bucket lid once each on cardboard and wrong side of jeans and 4 times on batting. Cut out cardboard and batting circles just inside drawn circles. Cut out jeans circle 4" outside drawn circle.

3. Hot glue 2 batting circles, cardboard circle, then remaining batting circles to center top of lid. Center lid batting side down on wrong side of denim circle. Pulling denim taut and trimming denim to reduce bulk as necessary, hot glue edges of denim circle to inside of lip of lid.

PATTERNS

EASTER WREATH
(Page 15)

HAPPY EASTER TREAT CANS
(Page 13)

EYES

EAR

TEETH

LARGE EGG

SMALL EGG

EGG

EASTER GIFT BOX
(Page 16)

PETAL

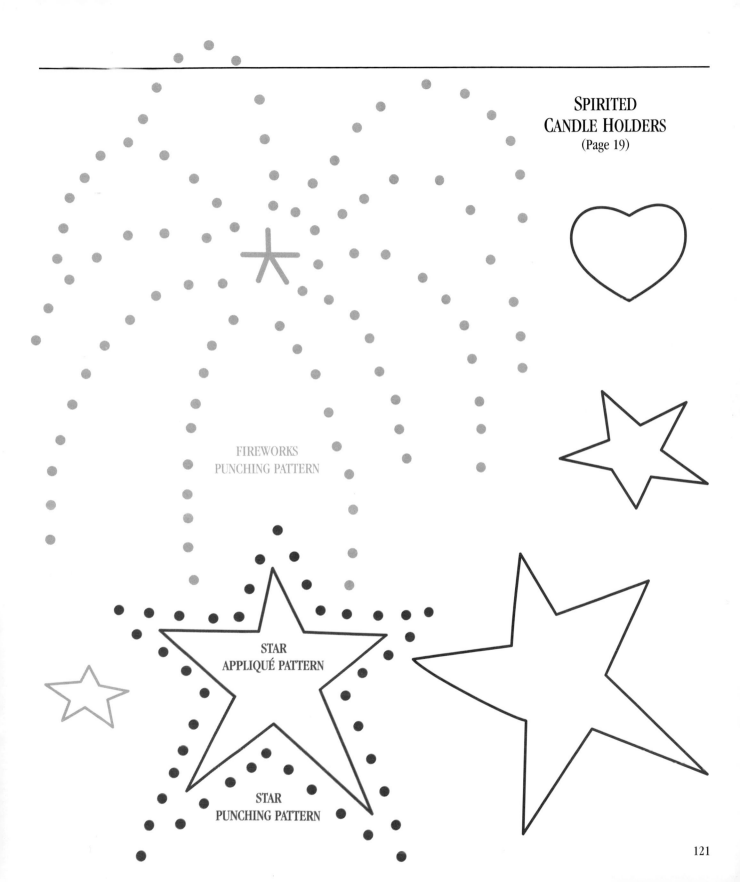

FIREWORKS
PUNCHING PATTERN

STAR
APPLIQUÉ PATTERN

STAR
PUNCHING PATTERN

121

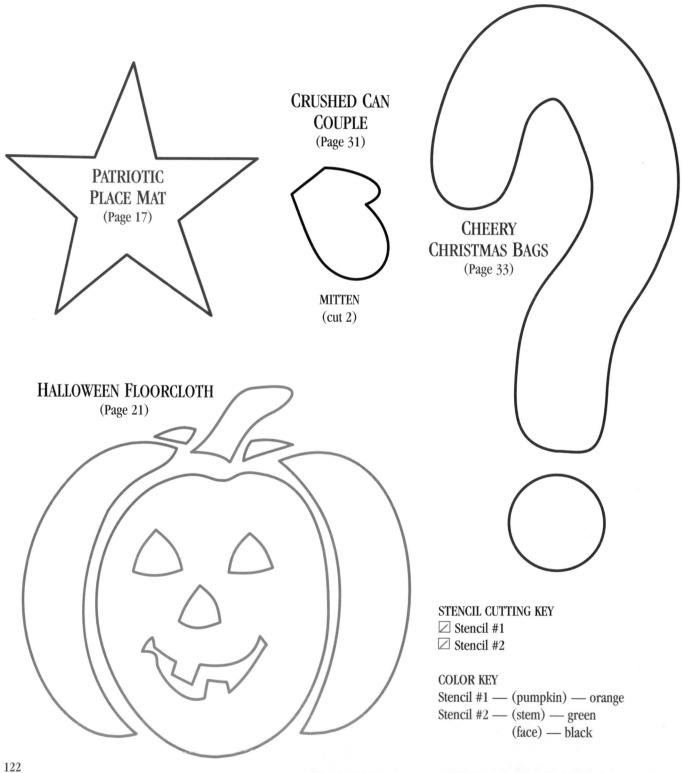

PATRIOTIC
PLACE MAT
(Page 17)

CRUSHED CAN
COUPLE
(Page 31)

MITTEN
(cut 2)

CHEERY
CHRISTMAS BAGS
(Page 33)

HALLOWEEN FLOORCLOTH
(Page 21)

STENCIL CUTTING KEY
☑ Stencil #1
☑ Stencil #2

COLOR KEY
Stencil #1 — (pumpkin) — orange
Stencil #2 — (stem) — green
(face) — black

BURNISHED JEWELRY
(Page 43)

"HOME-MADE" LAMP
(Page 49)

TRIANGLE

DANGLES

ROOF

LEAF

BOW

(make 5)

CHIMNEY

CORD OPENING

LAMP OPENING

PATTERNS (continued)

GIFT CANISTERS
FOR TEACHERS
(Page 55)

FLORAL DELIGHT LAMP
(Page 86)

PANSY BAG AND CARD
(Page 57)

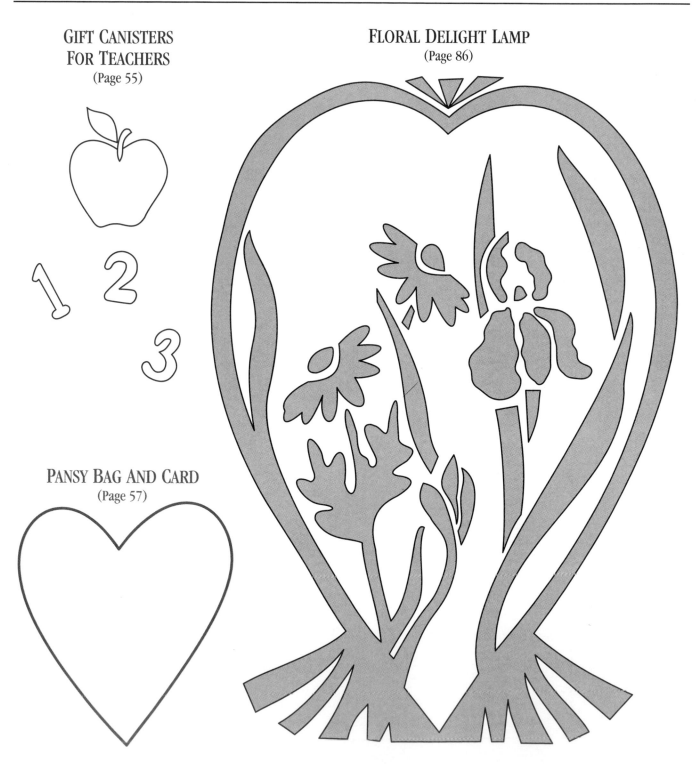

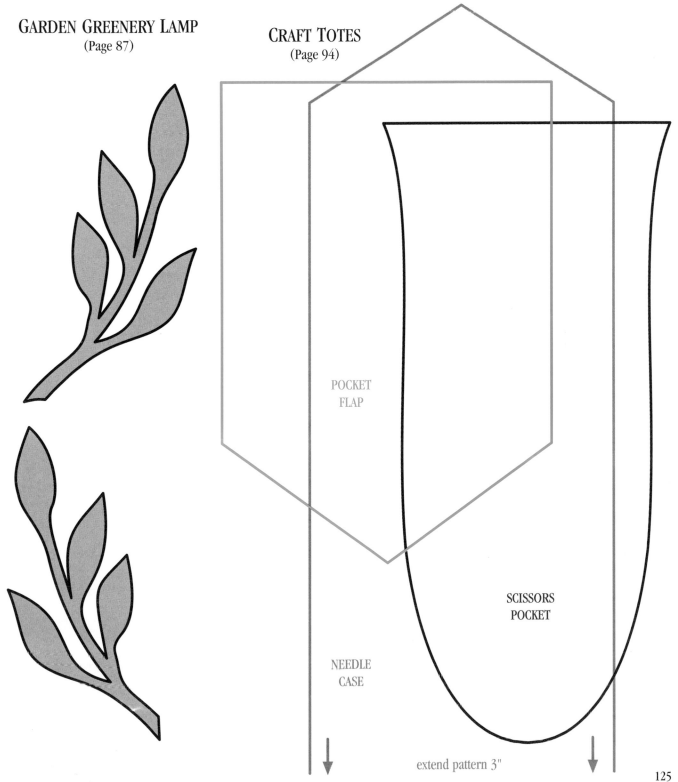

GARDEN GREENERY LAMP
(Page 87)

CRAFT TOTES
(Page 94)

POCKET
FLAP

SCISSORS
POCKET

NEEDLE
CASE

extend pattern 3"

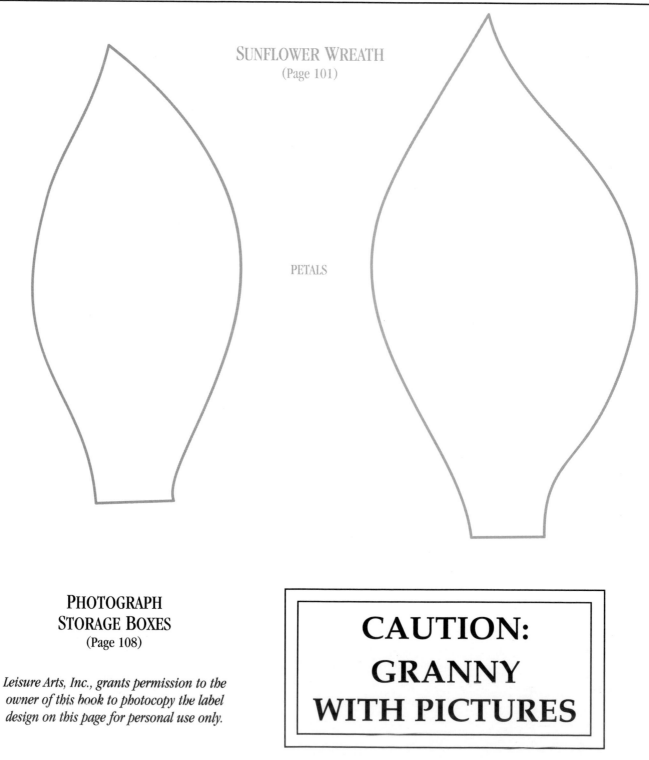

SUNFLOWER WREATH
(Page 101)

PETALS

**PHOTOGRAPH
STORAGE BOXES**
(Page 108)

*Leisure Arts, Inc., grants permission to the
owner of this book to photocopy the label
design on this page for personal use only.*

CAUTION: GRANNY WITH PICTURES

General Instructions

Tracing Patterns

Place tracing paper over pattern and trace pattern; cut out. For a more durable pattern, use a permanent pen to trace pattern onto acetate; cut out.

Sewing Shapes

1. Center pattern on wrong side of 1 fabric piece and use fabric marking pencil or pen to draw around pattern. DO NOT CUT OUT SHAPE.
2. Place fabric pieces right sides together. Leaving an opening for turning, carefully sew pieces together directly on drawn line.
3. Leaving a ¼" seam allowance, cut out shape. Clip seam allowance at curves and corners. Turn shape right side out.

Making A Multi-Loop Bow

1. For first streamer, measure desired length of streamer from 1 end of ribbon; gather ribbon between fingers (Fig. 1).

Fig. 1

2. For first loop, keep right side of ribbon facing out and fold ribbon to back to form desired size loop; gather between fingers (Fig. 2). Fold ribbon to

front to form another loop same size as first loop (Fig. 3). Continue to form loops, varying size of loops as desired, until bow is desired size.

Fig. 2

Fig. 3

3. For remaining streamer, trim ribbon to desired length.
4. To secure bow, hold gathered loops tightly. Bring a length of wire around center of bow. Hold wire ends behind bow, gathering all loops forward; twist bow to tighten wire. Arrange loops and trim ribbon ends as desired.
5. If bow center is desired, wrap a 6" length of ribbon around center of bow, covering wire and overlapping ends at back; trim ends. Hot glue to secure.
6. If fraying ends are a problem with the ribbon you've chosen, apply liquid fray preventative to cut edges of light to

medium weight ribbon or fabric glue to cut edges of heavy fabric or mesh ribbon.

Melting Wax

(*Caution:* When melting wax, do not place can directly on burner.) Cover work area with newspaper. Place can in pan on stove (or in electric frying pan); fill pan with water. Melt candle pieces in can to depth indicated in project. If necessary, add either Candle Magic® wax crystals or paraffin for more wax. If desired, remove paper from crayon pieces and add pieces to melted wax until desired color is achieved. If necessary, use a craft stick to stir wax.

Decoupage

1. Cut motifs from paper and arrange on item to determine desired placement. Remove motifs.
2. Use foam brush to apply a thin layer of glue to 1 area of item to be decoupaged. Brush glue lightly until it becomes tacky. Apply motifs to glued area; use fingertips or cloth to smooth out bubbles and wrinkles, working from centers of motifs outward. (*Note:* Some wrinkles will disappear as glue dries.) Use a damp cloth to gently remove excess glue. If motifs overlap, apply glue over placed motif, then place next motif on item. Repeat to apply remaining motifs. After applying all motifs, allow item to dry.
3. Apply 2 to 3 coats of clear acrylic spray to item to seal.

CREDITS

We want to extend a warm *thank you* to the generous people who allowed us to photograph our projects at their homes: Carl and Monte Brunck, Dr. Richard and Janie Calhoun, Leland and Georgiana Gunn, Shirley Held, Dr. Jerry and Gwen Holton, Carl and Marie Menyhart, Duncan and Nancy Porter, Linda Wardlaw, and Ron and Becky Werle.

Special thanks go to the I-40 Antique Mall of North Little Rock, Arkansas, for graciously supplying vintage accessories for some of our photographs.

To Magna IV Color Imaging of Little Rock, Arkansas, we say thank you for the superb color reproduction and excellent pre-press preparation.

We especially want to thank photographers Mark Mathews, Larry Pennington, Karen Shirey, and Ken West of Peerless Photography, and Jerry R. Davis of Jerry Davis Photography, all of Little Rock, Arkansas, for their time, patience, and excellent work.